Community Resources in the School Library Media Center

Concepts and Methods

W. BERNARD LUKENBILL

LIBRARIES
UNLIMITED
A Member of the Greenwood Publishing Group

Westport, Connecticut • London

Library of Congress Cataloging-in-Publication Data

Lukenbill, W. Bernard.
    Community resources in the school library media center : concepts and methods /
W. Bernard Lukenbill.
      p. cm.
    Includes bibliographical references and index.
    ISBN 1–59158–110–9 (alk. paper)
      1. School libraries—Collection development—United States. 2. Instructional materials
centers—Collection development—United States. 3. Libraries—Special collections—
Community information files. 4. Libraries and community—United States.
5. Community information services—United States. 6. Internet in school libraries—
United States. I. Title.
    Z675.S3L8954 2004
    025.2′1878—dc22   2004048926

British Library Cataloguing in Publication Data is available.

Library of Congress Catalog Card Number: 2004048926
ISBN: 1–59158–110–9

First published in 2004

Libraries Unlimited, 88 Post Road West, Westport, CT 06881
A Member of the Greenwood Publishing Group, Inc.
www.lu.com

Printed in the United States of America

The paper used in this book complies with the
Permanent Paper Standard issued by the National
Information Standards Organization (Z39.48–1984).

10 9 8 7 6 5 4 3 2 1

Acknowledgments

Line illustrations by Richard H. Hendler.

This book is dedicated to my grandmothers,
Mary Elizabeth Johnson McCorkle and Mattie Jane Smith Lukenbill.
I knew them only for a short time, but their memories are forever with me.

Contents

Illustrations

Acknowledgments

I owe many persons heartfelt thanks for all the help they have given me during my work on this book. My wife, Shirley Lukenbill, read all the pages of this manuscript. My son James took time from his doctoral studies to help me with research design and analysis. My grandson Aaron was there just to offer me his smiles. Richard, my illustrator, accommodated me with skilled diplomacy during my many mind changes as this book progressed. Appreciation is extended to the School of Information, University of Texas at Austin, for the support it extended to me through the Commons Teaching Fellowship. To all of these—Thanks!

Introduction

Community is central to life in the complex society of the twenty-first century. Community and community information pervade everyday existence, yet we in education and school-based information services do not often know how to integrate community information into the school environment and to use community resources effectively to increase student learning. This book lays a foundation for understanding the role of community information within the school library media center through models for services and development. These models and guidelines provide guidance to school media library specialists in the better use of community resources both as instructional and informational materials and as means for promoting student learning in a variety of subject areas.

School library media center specialists have always been interested in resources from the community and, along with their teacher-colleagues, have used community resources when appropriate to support informational needs and learning activities. One good example of this is the vertical file, or information file, that traditionally has held a great deal of community information, ranging from biographical to local history. I remember how impressed I was at my first position as a school library media specialist to discover that a former librarian many years before me had collected clippings and other materials about the school's involvement in the World War II effort. Before me lay a collection of community information about the school's "Victory Garden" and collection programs, such their scrap metal collection, activities all devoted to winning the war. This collection offered an outstanding contemporaneous view of the war efforts and the school's involvement in them.

A few years ago, I had a student who was doing a school library media center practicum in a middle school, and the major assignment was to develop a project that identified a problem that existed in the school library media center and to suggest practical solutions to resolve it. This student, working with the school nurse and counselor, decided that more information was needed about pregnancy prevention. For this project, a variety of printed community information resources was collected and organized with appropriate subject headings and placed in the vertical file.

Since that time, the Internet and the World Wide Web (WWW) have come to play a fundamental role in how information is designed, presented, and acquired. School media center specialists now have a vast array of community information in many formats at their fingertips. The question now is how to select, organize, and teach the use of these resources.

Terence Brake conducted research on library-based community information in schools for the British Library in the late 1970s. His study, published in the early 1980s, made numerous suggestions as to how community information could be organized and used in British schools. Although information technology has far surpassed what Brake recommended, his model is still viable today. In fact, it may be the only holistic model to consider how community information can be integrated into both a school library media collection programs as well as the school's instructional program. In supporting the value of community information in curriculum and instruction, Brake emphasized its role in developing information literacy.

The models offered in this book are informed by experiences in the field, by the expert opinions of school media center specialists, and by academic and professional theory and rational. The experiences of public libraries in providing community information also play an important part in this book, as they provide examples of successful community information programs suitable for adaptation and use in the modern school library media center.

Specifically, this book will consider:

- The concepts and theories that justify community information in the school library media center.
- How to determine and provide rationale for the value of community information in promoting learning and information literacy.
- How community information can be defined and collected.
- How to use networking to develop community information resources for the school library media center.
- How to organize a community information collection and program, using both traditional means of organization and new information technologies, such as the Internet and web-based designs.

- How to design and manage a community information program, including its financial and political support.
- How to recognize problems in collecting community information, such as content suitability, readability, and conceptual and age appropriateness.
- How to defend community information from censorship.
- How to market the community information program both internal to the school and to appropriate external communities.
- How to place community information into a multicultural context.

I hope that the models, professional opinions and theories, and practical suggestions made in this book will both inform and encourage school library media center specialists to move ahead with this exciting avenue of information so vital in our complex and changing world.

CHAPTER 1

Community and the School Library Media Center

INTRODUCTION: WHAT IS COMMUNITY?

Hillary Rodham Clinton used the old African proverb "It takes a village to raise a child" to emphasize the importance of community in the lives of modern-day children and youth. Her use of this reinforces the truism that individuals are connected through community and social life.[1] She begins her book, *It Takes a Village*, with a quote from Herman Melville:

> We cannot live for ourselves alone. Our lives are connected by a thousand invisible threads, and along these sympathetic fibers, our actions run as causes and return to us as results.[2]

In his travels in the United States in the 1830s, French scholar Alexis de Tocqueville observed that community life in America was vibrant. In terms of the enhancement of democracy, he particularly noticed and applauded the prevailing concept of direct local or community involvement and the role that volunteerism played in the life of American communities.[3] He saw it as one of the hallmarks of democracy in America.

Observation tells us that, today, American culture continues to place a high value on community and on sustaining strong community values through active involvement and volunteerism in one's community. American institutions, such as schools and libraries, are expected to foster this development through their instructional and service programs and to also actively encourage participation in community life.

Sociologists began to seriously study communities in the late nineteenth century, and today, as we move into the twenty-first century, those early studies continue to influence our thinking about community life. Early sociological concepts defined communities in territorial terms, noting that community has well-defined geographical locations and boundaries. Generally, this concept of community is connected with many positive attributes, such as solidarity, familiarity, unity of purpose, interest, and identity.[4] Today, theories about communities have been expanded or reformulated to include the idea that community is "a state of mind—collective sharing of an understanding or underlying feeling of sameness and belonging regardless of geographic location."[5]

In the 1980s, the "Chicago" school of social theory focused on understanding the impact of modernization on community development and structures, including urban culture, subculture, and society.[6] Since the beginning of the industrial revolution in the early nineteenth century, modernization has introduced a multitude of economic and social issues and problems that have challenged traditional assumptions about community and social arrangements. Some argue that because of social uncertainty, community can offer some relief from the turmoil of modernization by providing a sense of purpose and a framework for individual prosperity.[7] This need for community structure and identity significantly explains how community is taught and supported in today's schools and how it supports community information within the school library media center.

THE SCHOOL CURRICULUM AND COMMUNITY

The American and Canadian school curricula have traditionally assumed some responsibility for teaching about communities and the important role that individuals must play in maintaining a viable democratic society. School curricula for younger children stress the importance of the neighborhood and the people in a child's immediate environment. Curricula for older youth continue to do this, but they also introduce some of the complexities of social life and emphasize the importance of personal involvement in and responsibility for community. Work roles and economic opportunities that are available in the community are likewise introduced. Secondary curricula often continue this but may introduce critical analysis skills directed at helping youth probe some of the larger social issues that plague modern life. There is some argument concerning the role that critical analysis plays in community life instruction. One school of thought holds that instruction must continue to stress personal responsibility and loyalty to the community, state or province, and nation. The other view maintains that a well-informed citizen must be taught early to consider information about one's environment and to use that information in meaningful ways to understand problems and to make well-informed choices about social change. This theory holds that community instruction must stress the responsibility of the individual to encourage and participate in actions to correct perceived social problems or wrongs.[8]

Information Power, the standards for exemplary school library programs and services established by the American Association of School Librarians and the Association for Educational Communications and Technology, recognizes the role that families and communities play in students' learning. The standards note the value of community resources, such as the public library, museums, government agencies, and other private and social agencies, as sources for information. The standards maintain that collaboration, networking, and links with these as well as business and civic organizations are fundamental to good learning and to the development of good citizenship.[9]

The standards imply that professional involvement in community and community resources is not only necessary for curriculum development and the promotion of student learning, but it is also a way for professionals, such as school library media specialists, to address some of the pressing social needs affecting youth in our time. Social critic Joseph Illick writes that American children in most social classes at the end of the twentieth century were victims of the unequal distribution of wealth. Because of the necessity for a two-wage family income, many children from all classes were subjected to absent parents, thus depriving them of much needed nurturing and guidance. This, he notes, was particularly harmful to children in the inner city and rural areas. He contends that, in these areas, a nineteenth-century model of family life continued with its characteristics of poverty, family instability, and corporal punishment.[10]

Although *Information Power* does not speak directly to the needs for emotional family support and counseling within the school library media program, it does discuss the place of family in programming through the attention it gives to collaboration with parents and family in promoting information literacy and in helping to connect parents and families to information technologies.[11]

A tradition does exist within school library media center librarianship of connecting the library program to counseling and personal support through information. Early textbooks on school library management mentioned that providing job and career information (good examples of community information) as well as reader advisement were expected responsibilities of the school librarian.[12]

COMMUNITY RESOURCES

In general terms, community information is information that exists within a community environment. This can be in the local neighborhood, the city, county, or any other geographically defined area. It is often nonbibliographic in nature and may come from various sources, including individuals, agencies, groups, and businesses. As mentioned, school library media centers have always recognized that community resources are important to their collection and services, but because provision of such services has not been uniformly provided, this service has not received the attention that it deserves.

The best example of how community resources have traditionally been integrated into library programs and services is the vertical file, or information file. The Newark Public Library began its vertical file system early, and through the publication of its list of subject headings, it has undoubtedly influenced the development of the vertical file as a standard feature in libraries. The library's subject headings lists, published from 1917 to 1956, were particularly useful in providing a guide for local community subject headings that could be easily modified for other localities. Not only did Newark provide guidance in subject heading construction, but it also suggested how and where to find community information ranging from biographical information to information about local cultural and governmental affairs.[13]

The Hennepin County (Minnesota) Public Library is an excellent example of how community information has progressed well beyond the vertical file and has been integrated into the public catalog. Early in the 1970s, this library decided that because standard subject heading lists, such as Library of Congress (LC), were not adequate to reflect the richness of community resources or to serve the information needs of citizens, new subject headings were needed. Based on this rationale, the library developed an internal subject heading list that reflected its view of local community needs. From there, the library developed catalog records that not only described traditional library book and nonbook holdings but also created records that described community information and services.[14]

New information technology, such as the Internet, and information designs, such as web pages and the development of MARC records to accommodate community information, have likewise helped move community information into the mainstream of library information systems.[15]

Louis Shores, reference authority, encyclopedia editor, and a former dean of the Library School at Florida State University, recognized the vertical file, or information file, as a viable source and provided suggestions for its construction and management in his early editions on reference sources and services.[16] Margaret Rufsvold, founding dean of what is now the School of Library and Information Science, Indiana University, in her book on the management of audiovisual materials in the school library, likewise included community information as audiovisual materials, along with maps and globes. Unlike Shores, who emphasized the reference value of the file, she directed her attention to this community file as a vehicle for curriculum support. She was particularly interested in seeing that school librarians of the day understood that the curriculum reached well beyond the classroom and that librarians played a key role in making the connection between school and community. She advised school librarians to keep a systematic record or file of appropriate sites for field visits, persons in the local community who had interesting collections of artifacts for sharing, and, of course, persons who would be willing to come to the school as guest speakers or performers. The recording and dissemination of this information was to be carefully maintained through a file system made accessible through appropriate subject headings. Records in this file would include such items as contact names, a description of the source or site, special needs such as admission fees, and recommendations by a teacher who had experience with the source.[17] Later writers, such as Davies and Van Orden, continued to discuss the community information file as a central service to be provided by school libraries.[18]

INFORMATION AND REFERRAL SERVICES

In the 1960s and 1970s, both in this country and abroad, public libraries began to pay more attention to their roles in providing community information and formalized information and referral (I&R) services. A generally agreed on definition of I&R service follows:

> [T]he process of linking an individual with a need to a service or a source of information or advice which can fill that need. In providing this service, libraries must provide information and referral on several levels and by various methods.[19]

Most public libraries have no problem in providing descriptive and directory-type community information. The problem appears to be that, in providing I&R service based on the above definition, some public librarians see a conflict in roles. The question often asked is:

> By providing community information that requires advocacy or counseling support, is the library moving from its traditional politically neutral role to one of social activism?

I&R services that have their base in social work agencies typically have been expected to offer advocacy and counseling support for their clients along with information. Although many librarians have rejected this aspect as not being appropriate for public libraries, the American Library Association through the Public Library Association's guidelines of 1986 cited above gave its support to a limited advocacy role for libraries. Because of school media center librarians' close association with their students and their working relationships with counselors and other personnel, such as principals and school nurses, it is likely that community information provided in a school library situation will require an even more direct role in advocacy and counseling.

As mentioned previously, the theoretical literature of school media librarianship has supported the concept of community information, but the idea had not been widely implemented by the end of the twentieth century. As the twenty-first century unfolds, social, technological, and education changes now at work are likely to bring community information more forcefully into the service and program paradigm of the school library media center.

RATIONALE FOR COMMUNITY INFORMATION IN THE SCHOOL LIBRARY MEDIA CENTER

Information technology has made possible a global world where a "vast array of virtual communities" exists. Information technologies provide networks that bring people together and enable them to interact in a variety of ways, both publicly and privately.[20] Community information has many of those same network attributes.

Although school media librarianship has long recognized the importance of community life and the value of information in promoting critical thinking skills and literacy, there have been reasons for community information's slow development as a service in school library media centers. It is time-consuming, it must be justified within the framework of a school's mission and objectives, and it is expensive to develop in terms of initial program planning. The identification, verification, recording, and transmission of information is likewise labor-intensive. In some ways, the growth of the World Wide Web and its fast assortment of community information have made this somewhat easier in that many of these sources are already available. Another positive attribute is that most of the appropriate resources have been developed by reputable governmental and organizational sources, and their access and use simply require appropriate linkage through the media library center's web page. These problems are real, but using community information as a source for promoting youth success is a compelling reason for the inclusion of community information in the school library media center.

Recognizing the importance of community information and networking of resources, the Institute for Museum and Library Service (IMLS) through its programs of grants has encouraged museums and libraries to make available to the wider community many of their special resources. This often takes the form of digitizing resources and mounting them as web-based formats special items.[21] The Library of Congress, through its "American Memory" website, is an excellent example of how libraries with appropriate financial support can become a forum for public access to unique information resources (http://memory.loc.gov/).

The IMLS has used a cooperative program model to promote the integration of community and library, whereby mutual interests are served through joint programming. For example, the Houston Public Library (HPL) and the Houston Children's Museum (HCM) together have developed a program with grant support of IMLS in which each, based on common missions and goals, contributes some of its resources to a specific client group. In this case, the client group is the children of Houston. The HCM offers museum programs for children and maintains a parent resource library of quality materials in its quarters. The HPL permits these materials to be checked out from the collection using its library card, and books may be returned through branch libraries.[22]

The Northwest Regional Educational Lab in Portland, Oregon, has developed a community model that is built around the idea of "what makes for youth success." This program is designed to promote youth success by connecting schools, families, and communities. Questions raised in this model that are helpful to school library media center specialists as they reach out in their communities are how can youth success within communities be defined; how can characteristics that make for youth success in their communities be determined; how can youth be encouraged to develop characteristics that will make them successful within community life; what programs are necessary to promote the development of these characteristics; how can networking be conducted within the community to identify sources and talents; how can community assets be mapped; how can youth success be measured; what kinds of specific programs will promote youth success; and, finally, how can youth themselves be involved in program and project planning?[23]

MODELS FOR DEVELOPMENT

For various historical and social reasons, the public libraries in the United States, Great Britain, Canada, Scandinavia, and other English-speaking countries have a long history of involvement with community program development. Outreach or extension programs that many public libraries operate are good examples of community involvement. In recent years, this work has intensified due to concerns within society about parenting skills, the perilous status of many children, low literacy rates, immigration patterns, and increasing poverty rates among segments of the population. School library media specialists are often involved in such public library programming.

In some cases, school librarians have developed their own outreach programs. The most common types of outreach programs offered by school media libraries are parent collections and resources; parent circulation privileges; extended library hours, including summer hours; cooperation with local public libraries in programming; the development of web pages that include links to community as well as school information; and programs that connect the home to information technology services offered by the school.

Aside from these important services, access to community information and its role in the curriculum and instruction need to be given more consideration. In this regard, let us consider these questions:

- How can community information be better integrated into curriculum design?
- How can community information be used to promote critical thinking skills and the overall development of information literacy?

- How can community information be taught adequately?
- Who can and will teach community information?
- What materials are necessary for community information instruction?
- What place does community information have in government-mandated basic skills requirements?

THE BRITISH LIBRARY STUDY: A FIELD-TESTED MODEL

Similar questions were researched in a project sponsored by the British Library in the late 1970s. The project, under the direction of Terence Brake and reported in 1980, tested a curriculum unit that was developed to help students understand and better use community information in terms of their personal lives. The working definition of community information used in this study was information that could be easily found in students' neighborhoods and that could be used to help them better manage everyday problems. The study considered developmental and information needs of students as well as technical problems, such as how to locate appropriate information, how to organize it for access, and how to teach it within the existing structure of the centralized British school system. The study concluded that the school library media center could indeed play an important role in providing community information to students.

The study reported that, in developing this system, the school should begin with the local public library but should also include other community organizations. Information delivery systems would include bulletin boards, a community information file with appropriate subject headings, a pamphlet or literature counter containing items for free distribution, a small local reference section, and a collection of local directories.

As this study was completed well before the introduction of computers in school library media centers, it is easy to see how most of the suggestions can be accommodated through new information technologies.

Figure 1.1 suggests how a modern school library media information center might look based on the British model as just described.

Although teachers involved in the study felt that the unit of instruction was valuable and students seemed to benefit from it, the central problem they faced in terms of implementation was that the content was not a part of the centralized British national testing program, and teachers were pressed to find time for it within the time given to them for daily instruction.[24] Mandatory national and regional testing of students for specific skills that does not include community information is a problem to be faced by all who support community information as a legitimate instructional need and goal. New American federal and state requirements for the testing of basic skills raise similar questions.

Figure 1.1 Artist Concept of a School Library Media Community Information Center

CONCLUSION

The world is global, multicultural, and complex. The role of the school library media specialist reflects this through its growing multidimensional service aspects. This role requires that the school librarian be a specialist in many areas, ranging from curriculum to information resources to information technologies.

As in the past, social and cultural forces continue to place new demands on all institutions. Central to this is community and the role that individuals play in building community and in personally assuming responsibility for a democratic society. Educational systems play a vital role in socializing youth into community life and into democratic culture. Within the educational systems, school librarians stand at a unique place now. We have a history that is socially and historically progressive, an education that is conceptually sound, a social mission that is modern, and skills that have been tested and continue to improve. This means that school library media specialists are equipped to bring community information more forcefully into the school environment. This new role can only enhance our effectiveness as influential professionals working for the success of youth. The following chapters are designed to help bring this about.

NOTES

1. Hillary Rodham Clinton, *It Takes a Village: And Other Lessons Children Teach Us* (New York: Simon & Schuster, 1996), 12.

2. Ibid., 7.

3. Alexis de Tocqueville, *Democracy in America* (Chicago: University of Chicago Press, 2000).

4. D. Rabinowitz, "Community Studies: Anthropological," in *International Encyclopedia of Social and Behavioral Sciences*, ed. Neil J. Smelser and Paul V. Baltes, vol. 4 (Amsterdam: Elsevier, 2001), 2387.

5. Ibid.

6. Ibid.

7. B. D. Jacobs, " Community Sociology," in *International Encyclopedia of Social and Behavioral Sciences*, ed. Neil J. Smelser and Paul V. Baltes, vol. 4 (Amsterdam: Elsevier, 2001), 2383.

8. W. Bernard Lukenbill, *Collection Development for a New Century in the School Library Media Center* (Westport, Conn.: Greenwood Press, 2002), 148–49, citing E. Wayne Ross, "The Struggle for the Social Studies Curriculum," in *The Social Studies Curriculum: Problems, and Possibilities*, ed. E. Wayne Ross (Albany: State University of New York Press, 1997), 6–7.

9. American Association of School Librarians and Association for Educational Communications and Technology, *Information Power: Building Partnerships for Learning* (Chicago: American Library Association, 1998), 124.

10. Joseph E. Illick, *American Childhoods* (Philadelphia: University of Pennsylvania Press, 2002), 162–63.

11. American Association of School Librarians and Association for Educational Communications and Technology, 124, 12–27, 129.

12. Lukenbill, 6–7.

13. Miriam Ogden Ball, comp., *Subject Headings for the Information File*, 8th ed. (New York: H. W. Wilson, 1956).

14. Hennepin County Library, *[HCL] Catalog Bulletin* (Edina, Minn.: The Library, 1973, 1999. See also their *Cumulative Authority List* (Minnetonka, Minn.: The Library, August 5, ca. 1979, 1993).

15. *MARC 21 Format for Community Information; Including Guidelines for Content Designation.* Prepared by Network Development and MARC Standards Office, Library of Congress in cooperation with Standards and Support, National Library of Canada, 1999 ed. (Washington, D.C.: Library of Congress; Ottawa: National Library of Canada, 1999).

16. Louis Shores, *Basic Reference Sources* (Chicago: American Library Association, 1954), 227–28.

17. Margaret I. Rufsvold, *Audio-Visual School Library Service: A Handbook for Librarians* (Chicago: American Library Association, 1949), 53–54.

18. Ruth Ann Davies, *The School Library Media Center: A Force for Educational Excellence* (New York: R. R. Bowker, 1969), 78, 88–89. Ruth Ann Davies, *The School Library Media Center: A Force for Educational Excellence* 3rd ed. (New York: Bowker, 1979), 201–4. Phyllis Van Orden, *The Collection Program in Elementary and Middle Schools: Concepts, Practices, and Information Sources* (Littleton, Colo.: Libraries Unlimited, 1982), 78.

19. "Guidelines for Establishing Community Information and Referral Service in Public Libraries." Revised Edition of the 1980 Guidelines (revised January 1985), *Public Libraries* 25 (Spring 1986), 11–15. See also Public Library Association, *Guide-

lines for Establishing Community Information and Referral Services in Public Libraries, 4th ed. (Chicago: American Library Association, 1997).

20. Jacobs, 2385, citing M. Costells, *The Rise of the Network Society* (Oxford: Blackwells, 1996), 22.

21. Institute of Museum and Library Services and the University of Missouri-Columbia, "Web-Wise 2001—The Digital Divide: A Conference on Libraries and Museums in the Digital World," Washington, D.C., February 12–14, 2001.

22. Maureen White and others, "Great Things Come in Small Packages: A Parent Resource Library," *Journal of Youth Services in Libraries* 14 (Fall 2000): 8–11. Houston Public Library. "About the Parent Resource Library," n.d., available at www.hpl.lib.tx.us/youth/prl_about.html, February 5, 2003.

23. Diane Dorfman and others, *Planning for Youth Success: Resources and Training Manual, Connecting Schools, Families, and Communities for Youth Success* (Portland, Ore.: Northwest Regional Educational Laboratory, 2001). ERIC Reproduction No. 459 540.

24. Terence Brake, *The Need to Know: Teaching the Importance of Information. Final Report for the Period January 1978–March 1979.* (London: The British Library, 1980).

CHAPTER 2

Curriculum and Community Resources

INTRODUCTION

This chapter will consider the role of the curriculum in the modern school and how it shapes and influences both learning and the need for resources. The chapter will also further define community information and how it can be identified. Community sources will be considered, including political, social, and cultural resources available for a school library media center community information system. Resources, such as people in the community, community organizations, institutions, businesses, hotlines, crisis centers, and Internet resources, will be reviewed.

COMMUNITY, CURRICULUM, AND LEARNING IN THE MODERN SCHOOL

Curriculum is a cultural statement, and in the modern school it is designed to reflect what the society and culture of the nation, state, province, or locality that surrounds it see as important. Based on social and cultural expectations, curriculum within the school gives structure to what is selected for presentation to students and what is expected in the way of academic learning and positive social behaviors. Modern school communities in most countries have endorsed the importance of teaching civic goals and responsibilities. Early in their education, students are generally taught the framework of community life and how they fit into and use civil structure and community life. As students advance in their educational experiences, curriculum is generally broadened to include the role and responsibility of the individual within his or her community. In most societies, this includes emphasis on loyalty and patriotism to country. In democratic cultures, the role that the individual must play in fostering a democratic society is emphasized. With regard to this role, debate now centers on how to shape curriculum so that certain goals and objectives are met. As discussed in chapter 1, two major issues open to debate include these ideas: Should curriculum and instruction place emphasis on the role of the citizen to accept traditional concepts of government or should the goals of curriculum and instruction be given to educating students in critical thinking skills and in the astute use of information that empowers them to question social, cultural, and governmental directives?[1] National, state, and province agencies charged with educational control and oversight often mandate curriculum and instruction that endorse either one or both of these propositions.

Of course the debate about curriculum and instruction involves more than civil education. Education reform suggests numerous alternatives to traditional approaches to curriculum, instruction, and learning. It is not my intention to select and champion any one approach over another. Rather, my intention is to consider community information as a unifying and available resource that can serve a variety of approaches to learning and instruction. In doing this, I shall draw upon a variety of arguments— arguments that support the traditional approach as well as those that offer new approaches.

THE BRAIN AND HOW STUDENTS LEARN

Brain research in recent years has come to see the brain as a "pattern-seeking device." The brain does not have one component where logical operations are carried out; rather, it operates much like a complex computer. In solving an immediate problem, the brain constantly shifts through massive amounts of input data such as sight and sounds and remembered facts. By using multimodal paths, the brain then arrives at appropriate patterns suitable for solving the problem at hand. The brain seeks patterns in terms of objects, actions, procedures, systems, relationships, and situations. "Learning takes place when the brain sorts out patterns using past experiences to make sense out of input the brain receives."[2]

In 1983, Howard Gardner, in *Frames of Mind: Theory of Multiple Intelligences,* proposed that intelligence is more than just IQ. He saw intelligence as a means of producing something valued across all cultures. In his view, intelligence was "problem-solving and product producing." These areas of intelligence include logical-mathematical intelligence, linguistic intelligence, spatial intelligence, body-kinesthetic intelligence, musical intelligence, and intra- and interpersonal intelligences. All these intelligences operate independently of each other in different parts of the brain, but they must blend in the individual in order to produce a meaningful product. Gardner states that intelligence

> entails a set of problem-solving skills, enabling the individual to resolve genuine problems or difficulties that he or she encounters and, when appropriate, to create an effective product; it also entails the potential for finding or creating problems, thereby laying the groundwork for the acquisition of new knowledge.[3]

Educators Ross and Olsen maintain that learning comes from encountering complexities of the natural world. Learning is not necessarily fostered by deliberately oversimplifying natural phenomena for children in schools. They reject the idea that learning is best when topics are presented in neat, orderly, closely planned, and sequentially logical ways. They claim that brain research suggests that humans learn from "sense-making" or learning from the real world, which is rich, random, and sometimes chaotic.[4] Community information is one element of real life.

Ross and Olsen believe that good teaching comes from models that are pattern-seeking and based on multi-intelligence. Their preferred model relies on multiple resources for information and knowledge, such as government resources, organized advocacy groups, trade associations, foreign governments and their chancellors, professional groups, and individuals. Ross and Olsen recognize that public librarians with knowledge about community resources and directed by their mission of providing services facilitate the teacher's role in advancing the kinds of community-based resource teaching they endorse.[5] School media library specialists, through their knowledge of community resources, can play a role not only in this type of teaching, but they can also be involved in improving the more traditional type of teaching that occurs in many schools.

Although the Ross and Olsen model is interesting and helps to point out some important uses of community information, I do not intend to imply that it is the only model to follow. Community information, because of its breadth and versatility, has a place in many curricula and teaching approaches. The following section provides an overview of how community information can be used in teaching and in promoting learning.

CONCEPTS OF COMMUNITY INFORMATION

For the most part, definitions that we have for community information come from the public library. Generally, the definition found here is embraced by the concept of "Community Information and Referral." Clara S. Jones defined it in this way:

> Community information and referral consists of providing the community served and individual library users . . . with all pertinent information about and referral to sources that can provide answers to meet their needs for service and assistance.[6]

She considered community information to include governmental sources, community neighborhood and voluntary organizations, institutions, and individuals. She also limits this definition to the library providing information, not advice. More recent definitions of community information within the public library are not so conservative and suggest that the service, if not including advice, can certainly make referrals to sources where advice can be given.[7]

As mentioned in chapter 1, Louis Shores, in his 1954 textbook on reference sources, suggested that community information was indeed a legitimate information source and should be included as a part of the reference collection. Strange by today's terminology, he classified community information as audiovisual sources. He included as community information such items as all private and public agencies—schools, churches, newspapers, radio stations, businesses and industries, local government and welfare agencies, clubs, transportation agencies (bus, railroad, air transportation), and even natural resources found in the surrounding area. Shores suggested that it was the responsibility of the library staff to take an inventory of these resources and to prepare directories and indexes that would facilitate their accessibility and use.[8] William Katz noted that, in more recent times, even the most traditional libraries provide community resources. They readily call upon individual experts as resources and provide files, pamphlets, and booklists that provide useful community and personal-needs information. In so doing, libraries often become identified by groups within the community as information clearinghouses.[9]

Likewise, as mentioned in chapter 1, Margaret Rufsvold, Ruth Davies,[10] and Phyllis J. Van Orden[11] defended the importance of community resources as instructional tools. Speaking directly to the use of community information in the school library media center, Rufsvold placed particular emphasis on field trips or "school journeys" into the community and the use of human resources found in communities.[12] In their book on audiovisual instruction, James Brown and his co-authors described community resources similar to how a public library might view community information, but they placed less emphasis on personal information needs and advisement, concentrating on how community information can enhance student learning.[13] In her 1979 edition, Davies also gave considerable attention to how community resources could be integrated into social sciences instructional areas.[14]

EXAMPLES OF COMMUNITY INFORMATION IN CURRICULUM AND INSTRUCTION

Numerous examples of teaching units and exercises exist showing how community information plays a role in modern instruction. The following are two examples for younger children:

- *Members of Our Community.* Brandy Knieriem, a student at the University of Pittsburgh at Johnstown, developed an instructional unit designed to instruct students in grades 2 and 3 about the many different members and professional groups found in a community. Her emphasis focused on helping students to understand what it means to be a good and helpful community member. Community information in this unit consisted of explaining the work roles found in each student's home, identification by students of helpers in the community, and a selection by students of community buildings that can be used to build a classroom collage.[15]
- *The United States Postal Service.* Lora Jones and her colleagues developed a unit to teach students in grades 1 and 2 to better understand and appreciate the operations of the United States Postal Service. Community information suggested in this unit consisted of a field visit to the local post office to observe how mail is sorted for delivery to their homes, followed up by having the students create an in-class post office. In this unit, the book *The Jolly Pocket Postman* by Janet and Allan Ahlberg is used to demonstrate the variety of people in the community that a postman meets along his route.[16]

The following examples are for older students:

- *GI Bill.* South Stanley High School, Norwood, North Carolina. This unit, developed by Greg Speight, is for high school seniors in American history. It is a small two-hour unit and is designed to acquaint students with the GI Bill's creation and ramifications. In terms of community resources, the unit requires students to write a brief paper, locating and interviewing someone in the community who benefited from the GI Bill.[17]
- *Exploring Musical Instruments Using the Internet (The National Anthem).* This unit, created by Michelle Johnson for grades 6 through 8, is designed to teach students about musical instruments, musical sounds, and compositions for instruments. One aspect of the unit is to teach knowledge about the United States national anthem—its words, its sounds, and how it is to be honored. Activities include researching music on the Internet and requiring students to listen to the national anthem as recorded by local symphony orchestras, if available, or school bands.[18]
- *Marketing/Advertising Project.* Created by Tamara K. Johnson for use in senior-level general business and marketing classes, this plan calls for students to create a television advertisement as a project. For this preparation, students must visit television stations and businesses where television commercials are created.[19]

All these units have been designed to teach concepts that are enriched by resources found in the community. A review of such projects found on

"Teacher.Net" (www.teachers.net) suggests that these resources center on pictures, interviews, field visits, and use of the Internet. The assumption implied in most of these plans is that either the teacher or the student is responsible for locating the community resources required. Sometimes the school and public libraries are mentioned, but usually in regard to books and unspecified "resources."

School library media programs have responsibility for acquiring resources and helping teachers build units and make presentations such as those previously listed that are rich in the use of resources. Generally, this includes books, use of the Internet, and audiovisual materials. As noted earlier in this chapter, authorities in school media center management have long understood that community resources need to be among that array of resources. Implications drawn from a review of teaching units suggest that the overall assumption made by teachers is that they and students, not school library media specialists, are primarily responsible for locating community resources.

COMMUNITY RESOURCES IN THE SCHOOL LIBRARY MEDIA CENTER

Traditionally, school library media centers have collected community resources such as pictures of various resources in the community, biographies of individuals, and pictures of institutions and activities. The picture file and the vertical file have a long and respected history in library use. Over the years, some school library media specialists have developed index files and other means of access to suitable field site visits and to individuals who are willing to give their time and expertise to appear before classes. The wide use of the Internet and its vast resources gives the school library media center an additional means of providing community resources.

Appropriate community resources are varied, and their organization and promotion requires several approaches. The following are community resources that are found in school library media centers:

- *The Picture or Graphics File:* The picture or graphics file is a file of appropriately selected pictures or graphics that have been collected for their usefulness in the school. In terms of community information, this may include pictures of buildings of historical, environmental, or architectural importance; people; and events. The pictures need to be appropriately mounted with archival quality materials and procedures and accessed through useful subject headings. Although it is somewhat outdated by today's concepts, Donna Hill provides fundamental suggestions on how to select, organize, and maintain a picture collection.[20] Electronic graphics need a different form of management, including indexing and retrieval mechanisms, that are computer based. Descriptions of inexpensive image viewers with indexing support are available from sources such as Tucows (http://mac.megalink.com).

- *The Vertical/Information File:* The vertical or information file also has a long and respected history. This file offers an easy and inexpensive way of collecting and making accessible various types of community resources. Because the vertical file is time consuming in terms of collecting materials and managing the system, some school library media specialists have felt that it is too expensive to maintain. Instead, some have decided to collect only community information. This might be defined as information relating to the school, the local area surrounding the school, a region of the city, or any locally defined area of interest. Once a collection policy has been developed and sources identified, the materials can be organized and arranged using a controlled vocabulary subject approach. Most of the available subject heading lists offer examples of local subject headings that can be adapted for local situations. Clara Sitter offers guidance on the construction of the vertical file through her book *The Vertical File and Its Alternatives.*[21]
- *Directories:* Directories can include school, organizational, city, county, phone, and government directories.
- *Indexes:* Indexes to specific community sources can include those found on the Internet as well as indexes that are produced by the school media library staff to satisfy specific access needs, such as indexes to local publications.
- *Materials for Distribution:* Most, if not all, organizations within communities produce free materials for distribution. This includes information on health, cultural and social events, recreation, and access to help of various kinds. Within the selection and acquisition of the school, the school library media center can encourage and facilitate access to this material by identifying, reviewing, collecting, and maintaining a distribution center for free items. This can often be done with the assistance of such school personnel as the office staff, the counselor's office, the food staff, and the school nurse.
- *Clipping and Posting Service:* Special libraries for many decades have maintained clipping services that routinely review selected print resources for specialized and hard-to-find information. A good example of this is the Texas Legislative Reference Library, which for years has maintained a clipping program that routinely reviews major national and regional papers, and clips and files articles that pertain to the legislative interests of legislators (http://www.lrl.state.tx.us/research/clips/lrlhome.cfm). In accordance with the school selection and acquisition policy, a school library media center staff can also review and clip items from selected local newspapers, magazines, and other publications. These clippings can be placed in the vertical file, the picture file, or posted on a bulletin board as appropriate.
- *Internet Resources:* The Internet offers an abundance of materials. Community information is provided by cities, school systems, organizations, newspapers, radio and television stations, trade organizations, and other entities that have an interest in promoting aspects of the local community. Most have individual websites and can be located through web browsers such as Netscape Navigator and Microsoft Internet Explorer. Search engines such as Google.com are also useful. Subject access to these sites varies, but once a city or regional site is found, the indexing system can point out links to appropriate sites within the area. Public libraries often will offer links to these resource sites through their own websites. Following selection and acquisition policies of the school, the most useful and appropriate of these can be bookmarked by the school library media staff and made

available to teachers and students through convenient directories. The school library media center can often mount appropriate sites on its own web page for easy access.

- *In-House Information Production:* School librarians have always had opportunities to be producers of information resources. They create bibliographies, find guides, make reading lists, and even take pictures of events happening in the school. With the advent of better technologies, these opportunities have expanded. Products of local information can now be created using the computer and appropriate programs such as PowerPoint, Front Page, and the various programs that create web pages. Photo editing programs, such as PhotoShop and less expensive programs like Ulead Photo Explorer, can help the inexperienced school media center librarian become a proficient graphic artist. PowerPoint presentations of local information (e.g., historic homes, contemporary buildings, landscapes, recreation areas) can be created by the library staff and made available to teachers and students as resources, and the school media library staff can create school and community scrap books and other forms of memorabilia. Many school librarians already videotape school events and programs, adding to community information available in the center. This means that now local experiences and information products can be created with a minimum level of expertise.

- *Archives:* All organizations produce archives and manuscripts in the course of their operation. Archives can certainly add to the depth of community information available in the school library media center. Archives do not contain everything that an institution might have produced. Collecting and assessing items coming into an archive must be based on well-understood missions, goals, and objectives that give direction to collection development. Based on careful acquisition and review consideration, a school archive can include materials created by school clubs and organizations and school-based events. The school archive might also include, on a selective basis, the archival materials produced by organizations in the local area of the school and those that have close ties to the school, such as a neighborhood recreation center or PTA. An easy-to-follow-and-understand guide that offers help in management of a small archival program is Elizabeth Yakel's *Starting an Archives.*[22]

- *Self-Help and Personal Information:* As mentioned earlier, public library community information and referral services have generally considered personal and life-coping information as a legitimate part of their responsibilities. Social service agencies that also provide information and referral services differ from libraries in that they generally consider the offering of advice, counseling, and advocacy as an important part of their responsibilities. Public libraries may indeed collect in such areas, but they offer advice on a very general level, restricting this to directional or referral levels. Following guidelines established by school policy and in cooperation with other school personnel, school library media center programs may collect and distribute information in such areas as well. This information may be in the form of information to be distributed, it may be listed in a directory, or it may be maintained on the school media center's website. The literature of information and referral services throughout the years has addressed such self-help and personal needs as the information needs of gays, lesbians, and bisexuals; adolescents, people in rural communities, and persons who suffer from physical and sexual abuse situations.[23]

CONCLUSION

Community information is varied and its use is widespread. Teachers make considerable use of it in lesson plans and presentations but often they are left to their own resources to find it. Although the school library media center is appreciated for its collections of books and audiovisual materials, it is not generally seen as a source for local or community information. Clearly, community information plays an important role in the learning of students, and because of this, school library media center specialists will want to expand their responsibility for collecting in this area. Not only does community information support curriculum, but it plays an important role in helping students develop information literacy skills and manage information in their everyday lives.

NOTES

1. E. Wayne Ross, ed., *The Social Studies Curriculum: Purpose, Problems, and Possibilities* (Albany: State University of New York, 1997), xi–xii.

2. Ann Ross and Karen Olsen, *The Way We Were… The Way We Can Be: A Vision for the Middle School Through Integrated Thematic Instruction*, 2nd ed. (Kent, Wash.: Books for Educators, 1993), 20.

3. Ibid., 15, quoting Howard Gardner, *Frames of Mind* (New York: Basic Books, 1983), 60–61.

4. Ross and Olsen, 24.

5. Ibid., 133.

6. Clara S. Jones, ed., *Public Library Information and Referral Service* (Syracuse, N.Y.: Gaylor, 1978), 29.

7. Public Library Association, Community Library Section, *Guidelines for Establishing Community Information and Referral Services in Public Libraries; with a Selected Annotated Guide to the Literature on Information and Referral*, 4th ed. (Chicago: Public Library Association and American Library Association, 1997), 15–16.

8. Louis Shores, *Basic Reference Sources* (Chicago: American Library Association, 1954), 227–38.

9. William A. Katz, *Introduction to Reference Work*, vol. 2, 8th ed. (Boston: McGraw-Hill, 2002), 33.

10. Ruth Davies, *The School Library Media Center: A Force for Educational Excellence* (New York: Bowker, 1969), 78–79, 88–89.

11. Phyllis J. Van Orden, *The Collection Program in Elementary and Middle Schools: Concepts, Practices, and Information Sources* (Littleton, Colo.: Libraries Unlimited, 1982), 78, 88–89.

12. Margaret I. Rufsvold, *Audio-Visual School Library Service: A Handbook for Librarians* (Chicago: American Library Association, 1949), 53–54.

13. James W. Brown, Richard B. Lewis, and Fred F. Harcleroad, *AV Instruction: Technology, Media, and Methods*, 6th ed. (New York: McGraw-Hill, 1983), 40–62, 364–65.

14. Ruth Davies, *The School Library Media Program: A Force for Educational Excellence*, 3rd ed. (New York: Bowker, 1979), 201–4.

15. Brandy Knieriem, "Members in Our Community," *An AskERIC Lesson Plan*, Lesson Plan # AELP-CIV020, January 24, 2001, available at http://askeric.org/Virtual/Lessons?Social_Studies/Civics/CIV0200.html.

16. Lora Jones, Pat Ganzy, Christy Bennett, Peter West, and Kim Sutton, "The United States Postal Service," *An AskERIC Lesson Plan*, Lesson Plan #: AELP-CIV0010, n.d., available at http://www.askeric.org/Virtual/Lessons/Social_Studies/Civics/CIV0010.html, January 29, 2003.

17. Greg Speight, "GI Bill," *Teachers.Net Lesson Bank*, #2178, March 16, 2001, available at www.teachers.net/lessons/posts./2178.html.

18. Michelle Johnson, "Exploring Music Instruments Using the Internet," *Welcome to LessonPlans.Com.*, n.d., available at www.lessonplanspage.com/MusicCIMDInstrumnetsSoundsComositionsNeet68.htm.

19. Tamara K. Johnson, "Marketing/Advertising Project," *Teachers.Net. Lesson Bank.* #1100, June 25, 1999, available at http://www.teachers.net/lessons/posts/1100.html.

20. Donna Hill, *The Picture File: A Manual and a Curriculum-Related Subject Heading List*, 2nd ed. (Hamden, Conn.: Linnet Books, 1978).

21. Clara L. Sitter, *The Vertical File and Its Alternatives: A Handbook* (Englewood, Colo.: Libraries Unlimited, 1992).

22. Elizabeth Yakel, *Starting an Archives* (Metuchen, N.J.: Society of American Archivists and Scarecrow Press, 1994).

23. "Continuing Bibliography of the Literature of Information and Referral," *Information and Referral*, 14 (1992 [to 1998?]) Apparently, the bibliography is no longer published. The bibliography was published first as the 1992 volume of the journal *Information and Referral*. It was intended to be an annual supplement to each subsequent issue. As of 1998, the full bibliography contained over 1,400 annotated items and at that time was maintained as a PRO-CITE electronic database. In 1998, copies were held by the U.S. National Information and Referral Support Center and the Alliance of Information and Referral Systems (AIRS) National Office. Source: *Library and Information Science Abstracts*, Accession number: 59967.

CHAPTER 3

Selection and Management

INTRODUCTION

As with the development of any collection, the selection of community resources is important and must be approached with care. This chapter will consider how to put a community resource collection management plan into place, how to identify and find suitable materials, and what selection issues are involved in the construction and management of a community information system. Specifically, the topics to be discussed include how to develop a community resources collection policy within the framework of existing management, what to consider as community resources, how to select from what is available, what review sources exist, what to expect in terms of challenged materials, and how to defend the collection from censorship.

BASIC MANAGEMENT PRINCIPLES: COLLECTION DEVELOPMENT

Numerous books and articles concerning the management of school library media collections have been written over the years. Some recent titles include Ken Haycock's (editor) *Foundations of Effective School Library Media Programs*,[1] Phyllis J. Van Orden and Kay Bishop's *The Collection Program in Schools: Concepts, Practices, and Information Sources*,[2] and Blanche Woolls's *The School Library Media Manager*.[3]

Several overriding themes emerge from these works. Central to all is planning. Collection development must be systematically planned and executed. A collection cannot be allowed to grow haphazardly. A collection development plan must be in place that will guide the collection's development over several years. The plan must consider many elements, including, but not necessarily limited to, curriculum needs and plans, instructional requirements, recreational needs and interests, literacy development, and social and cultural needs and expectations.[4] A collection development plan will include professional beliefs, theories, and judgments about what is right and needed for the collection. It will also include a time frame of how the collection plan will unfold and will consider a delineation of relationships, roles, and responsibilities. Likewise, for collection development, it will present a hierarchical framework that places the collection development plan within the structure of how policies and decisions are executed by the local school and the school system.

Professors Robert Stueart and Barbara Moran advise that all collection development plans must ask these questions:

- Why and for what purpose is the collection developed?
- Who will be involved in developing the collection?
- When and how will the plan be implemented?
- Where will the plan be executed?
- How will the plan be executed?[5]

In addition to having a plan, collection development must consider other important elements of management: institutional vision, mission, goals and objectives, and activities. Once developed, these provide stability and consistency for the collection development plan. Vision offers a conceptual and philosophical view of what to expect within the organization and how collection development advances the vision. The mission of an organization states in concrete terms expected goals, objectives, and activities. The mission statement of the school or school system helps the collection development plan find focus and direction. At the more concrete level, goals of the organization are statements of designs and aspirations, and they are expressed in terms of concrete operations, policies, strategies, and activities.[6]

Collection development plans draw heavily on the goals of the school and school system in terms of their internal structures. Essentially, collection development plans are official statements that encompass:

- designing plans of operation (management and lines of responsibility for the plan);
- developing and setting policies (constructing an overall method of operation);
- constructing strategies (developing structures so the plan can succeed); and
- formulating activities (establishing functions necessary for the plan's execution).

Community information can and must fall within the collection development plan of both the building-level school library media center as well as the entire school system.

COMMUNITY INFORMATION AND COLLECTION DEVELOPMENT

Like any type of information and materials acquired by the school library media center, community information and resources must meet requirements of the school library media center materials selection policies and guidelines. In this regard, such materials are no different from other materials acquired for the collection. For example, these materials must be age-appropriate. They must be conceptually sound in design and presentation so that the informational content is understood by the intended students; they must be accurate and present a clearly identifiable point of view; they must be up-to-date; they must be accessible and available; and they must meet the information or recreational needs of the students. Because of the nature of community information and resources, social agencies' and advocacy groups' information must be verifiable and authenticated in terms of official information and policies of the issuing body.

OPTIONS FOR COLLECTION DEVELOPMENT

Because community information is very broad in concept, school media specialists have several management options in terms of how to build their programs:

- *Community Information in the Vertical File or Archives Collection.* Collect community information, treat it as vertical file information, and provide access to it through an existing vertical file system with appropriate subject headings. Some community information may be considered archival material and maintained in an archive collection within the school library media center.
- *Community Information and Display.* Maintain a community information bulletin board that selectively displays information about the community.
- *Community Information and Curriculum Instruction.* Collect and provide access to community information that supports instruction and curriculum, paying particular attention to field sites and persons in the community who are willing to speak to classes.
- *Community Information and the Local Community.* Provide a collection that is carefully configured to contain highly selected information, such as sources found in the neighborhood of the school or information that exists in the larger community but is narrowly defined.
- *Community Information and I&R Services.* Provide community information that addresses human services that may include referral. This requires extensive knowledge of the school community and its needs, and it requires close association with

the school's administration and staff, such as counselors, nurses, and food directors. This type of program necessitates knowing about, collecting information on, and documenting human service agencies in the community where human service needs are addressed. Likewise, it means being able to access personal problems and needs and to make referrals to agencies where help can be given. Because of the personal and therapeutic nature of assessment and referral, it is best to work directly with the appropriate school staff, such as the school nurse, social worker, or counselor, rather than to make independent judgments and referrals. In this model, the school library media specialist assumes a support role. Under the guidance of the school library media specialist, community information is collected and organized based on school needs (including personal help information). In a consultative role, the media specialist provides that information to proper school staff members who are trained to work directly with clients and to make proper referrals.

THE COMMUNITY RESOURCES DIRECTORY

Definitions and Purpose

To avoid confusion, the term *directory* is used in this discussion to refer to the community resources file. As generally understood by human service agencies and public libraries that offer community information programs, the "community resources directory" is a file or directory that lists and briefly describes resources available within the community.[7] The Public Library Association's Community Information Section describes the directory as an "accurate and up-to-date file of organizations and services available to the public."[8]

Materials in a community resources directory within a community information program for a school library media center program must first meet the general mission, goals, and objectives of the school and the school's material selection policy. The fundamental objectives of the community resources directory are to provide needed information, meet curriculum needs, and promote student learning.

Management and Selection of Sources

Management and development decisions and guidelines for the directory must be carefully considered and developed. These guidelines must be

- consistently developed and applied, and the principles must be well understood by the staff;
- uncomplicated and easily applied;
- consistent with the school library media center's materials selection policy.[9]

These three characteristics are important not only for an orderly development of the resource directory, but they also can be used to support selection and inclusion decisions in the case of censorship or protest.

Selection of resources for the directory reflects local needs and conditions. Selection can give higher priority to one set of resources and subjects over others based on the local situation.[10] For example, a center might elect to gather materials more extensively on youth programs that address mental health needs of adolescents over resources that emphasize recreation. A school library media center may decide to focus its attention only on resources that address very specifically the needs of curriculum and instruction. For example, the directory might include primarily institutions that offer field trip experiences or that provide personnel for classroom appearances. Another program's directory might emphasize individuals in the community who have special talents or have special collections that they are willing to share with students at the school. Still another program might decide to include both in its directory.

Currency and stability of the resources are additional important considerations. The size of the directory is only secondary to the accuracy and currency of information that it provides. Large and extensive files generally present control and management problems. Selectivity based on understandable selection policies can ensure that the directory remains current, relevant, and accurate in terms of information provided and subjects covered.

Stability of resources must be carefully considered before they are listed. In terms of community groups or organizations, indicators of stability can include the existence of offices, telephone access, e-mail addresses, a website, or other means of providing contact.[11] Geographic coverage of resources located in the directory is important. As stated, the directory must reflect local needs; in many cases, local needs are based on geographic location. An issue to decide early in the planning stage is the geographic limits of coverage. Will the directory cover the entire state or province, the local governmental district, the entire school system, the city, or only the local area surrounding the school?[12] Terence Brake, in his study of community information in a British school, identified the local "casement" or geographic boundaries served by the school as a logical limitation for collecting community resources.[13]

Other selection considerations include the profit or nonprofit status of a listing. Some directories exclude "for-profit" groups. Other questions to consider are whether private practitioners, such as physicians and tax consultants, should be included; and whether certain groups that have specific membership exclusion clauses (or groups that are financially supported by organizations that have exclusion statements) be excluded from the directory. For example, should the Boy Scouts of America be excluded from the directory because of their rejection of gay youth and gay adult leaders? To ensure stability, some libraries and human services agencies require that groups that are listed in the directory have a paid staff (generally at least one paid staff member) before the group is included. Should political and issue-oriented or cause-advocacy groups be included? Should only groups that are visible or have longevity within the community be included?[14] These issues are not new to librarians who over the years have had to face similar situations when making materials selection decisions regarding collection development. In building the community information program and directory, the Library Bill of Rights; court rulings regarding censorship, especially *Board of Education, Island Trees, New York v. Pico* (457 U. S. 853); and the school library media center's materials selection policy will offer guidance.[15]

Acquiring Resources for the Directory

Resources for the directory file are numerous. The most obvious selection sources to be consulted are published directories that are already available in the community, such as the local phone directory. Usually, phone directories will list important government offices and agencies that warrant review consideration. More selectively, the Yellow Pages can offer a list of resources. Geographic areas such as larger cities now have phone directories that target local areas within the city or within other well-defined geographic areas. Specialized directories often exist in communities and include religious organizations, charity groups, and special-interests group. Specialized directories that list memberships in clubs, associations, and professional groups are also useful. Once resources are identified through these directories, they can be contacted and the information reviewed for inclusion. Information about the source can be acquired by telephone interview or by mailed survey. Figure 3.1 provides an example of how such information can be collected for systematic review.

The Internet and the widespread use of computers offer additional means of acquiring community directory resources. Most cities and other organized governmental areas of any size now have websites. These websites list government agencies and programs and will often include links to community and service groups in the area that advance the mission and goals of local government. School districts also have websites that provide public information, public relations, and promotional tools, and in this capacity, they chronicle their own missions and goals. As a part of information campaigns, they provide links and other information about the school district and its schools. They may also offer links to other closely allied community resources that reflect their own missions, goals, and interests.

Consider public libraries and other libraries in the community as sources of appropriate community information. Most, if not all, university and college libraries have websites, and they will often post links to community resources. Some public library websites not only list their own programs, but they also will offer links to and information about a wide variety of community resources.

Networking and "walking the neighborhood" offer both formal and informal means of identifying sources for the resources directory. Networking

COMMUNITY RESOURCES SURVEY

1. **Please check one of the following:**
   ___ Agency or Service Provider
   ___ Individual Provider (e.g,, parent, business person, etc.)

2. **Contact Information:**
   Address _____
   City _____ State _____ Zip _____
   Phone _____ Email _____
   Fax _____ Other Contact Information _____

3. **If organization, please check type:**
   ___Profit ___Non Profit _____

4. **If organization, please give contact information:**
   Name_____ _____
   Phone _____ Email _____
   Fax _____ Other Contact Information _____

5. **If Individual Provider, please given contact information:**
   Name of provider _____
   Address _____
   Email _____
   Fax _____
   Other Contact Information _____

6. **Describe services offered or talents to share:**
   _____
   _____

7. **Fees or contact specifications:**
   _____

8. **If service agency, give eligibility for services:**
   _____

9. **If service agency, state how services are obtained:**
   _____

10. **If service agency, give geographic areas served:**
    _____

11. **If individual, please describe talent(s) to share:**
    _____ collections
    _____hobbies
    _____ employment and career information
    _____ travel experiences
    _____ Other (please describe):

12. **In the space below please provide other information:**
    _____
    _____

For staff use: Date received _____ . Subjects/topics:_____
Notes:

Figure 3.1 Community Resources Survey

is important and is discussed in more detail in chapter 4. Networking is a means whereby the staff can personally connect with individuals and groups in the community. This can be done informally through contacts with friends and colleagues, or it can be a more formal approach whereby the school library media specialist develops and maintains contact through official channels with key personnel located in business, government, churches, organizations, and other institutions within the community.

Neighborhood walks (promoted by the Detroit Public Library) is a procedure used by some library staffs to help them become acquainted with their neighborhoods. It involves walking (or driving) through the neighborhood; learning about the businesses, organizations, and people there; and learning how they might contribute to the resources directory. The Detroit Public Library used this technique early in the development of its community information program; librarians personally canvassed neighborhoods looking for and documenting sources of community information.[16]

Questionnaires and talent surveys offer other ways of identifying resources for the directory. These approaches work well in a closed, clearly defined organization such as a school where an audience is easily targeted. For example, in a school, the library media specialist can develop a questionnaire or survey asking parents or others in the school community area to list their special interests, talents, hobbies, experiences, and collections and to indicate how they are willing to share those assets within the school. Responses from the questionnaires and surveys can then be reviewed and evaluated for inclusion in the directory file.

Documentation and Review

Although the previously mentioned procedures are useful in identifying possible resources for inclusion in the directory, systematic recording of data is important. Not all sources identified are appropriate for the directory, but in making judgments about their appropriateness, a systematic record must be made. This is very much like a consideration file for book selection. It lists items that must be taken into consideration before an item is entered into the directory. The following format provides suggestions as to what might be included on a community directory acquisition/consideration form (see Figure 3.2).

THE VERTICAL/INFORMATION FILE

The vertical/information file (sometimes called the pamphlet file) is another useful tool for providing community information. Although now in decline, it has been used by libraries for generations to provide access to

Community Resource File Assessment Form

Name of Establishment _____

Date of assessment _____

Contact information:
  Person to contact/or contacted _____
  Position _____
  Address _____
  Phone _____
  Email _____
  Fax no _____

  Other forms of contact

Type of Resource and/or Placement in Community Information File:
  _____ Field Trip/Site Visit
  _____ Consultant or Presenter
  _____ Service Agency
  _____ Printed or Audiovisual Resource
  _____ Archival Resource
  _____ Electronic Resource (website, CD, etc.)
  _____ Other

Description of Resource:
  (Include: nature of the resource, usefulness to the resources, audience focus, use in curriculum and instruction, and special features and services. For service agencies include services offered, hours of operation, fees, if any, edibility requirements, and a general description of the agency's services. Include recommendations, evaluations, and or reviews. Use back of page if necessary.

_____
_____
_____

Suggested subject headings/descriptors for file(s):

Figure 3.2 Community Information File Assessment Form

ephemeral materials. It is also used to provide information that is timely and that may not be readily available in other sources.

Access to Community Life

Its use for community information is even more focused in that it can be used to highlight community information. Traditionally, the information file has provided access to community information by using subject headings that help pinpoint community information. For example, Newark Public Library subject list, *Subject Headings for the Information File*, edited by Miriam Ball, established **N. J.** for state materials, **Essex Co.** for county materials relating to Essex County, New Jersey, and **Newark** for Newark city materials. The Toronto Public Library's *Subject Headings for Vertical Files*[17] and *Sears List of Subject Headings*[18] followed similar patterns.

In addition to geographic subject terms, the pamphlet file is generally organized around major subject headings with no bibliographic record of each item made. For this reason, subject headings for the pamphlet file can be adapted from standard subject headings lists, such as *Sears List of Subject Headings* and the *Vertical File Index*. For the most part, the subject approaches provided in these lists are created to support the needs of the general library community and may not exactly fit the requirements of the local situation. The local school library media center staff may need to adapt and maintain their own subject authority file.

Although useful in terms of suggesting structure and form, society and community information are much more complex than the terms that these lists provide. Recognizing this, in 1973, Hennepin County (Minnesota) Library began publishing its own subject headings list to meet the demands of both its community information service and the general library collection.[19] Through this mechanism, the library introduced such terms as **Crisis Centers and Switchboards, Rape Crisis Centers, Women's Shelters, Youth Shelters,** and **Hotlines, Crisis.**[20] Geographic subdivision rules in the list permitted selected terms to be specifically applied to community services and support systems within its service area. The subject heading **Youth Shelters—Hennepin County** is an example of this approach.

The Detroit Public Library TIP (The Information Place) service does not rely on library-based subject headings to index its community information directory. Instead, TIP uses a standardized list approved by the Alliance of Information and Referral Systems (AIRS). This list, *A Taxonomy of Human Services*[21] (also know as "The Info Line Taxonomy"), offers a common classification scheme that "facilitates the exchange of [human service] data between I&R providers."[22] It is designed to move from the general to the specific, and indexers can use the terms that best fit their needs.

Integration of Community Information

Integrating community information into the general vertical or information file may be the most appropriate way for smaller school library media centers to provide community information, but for centers that wish to place a special emphasis on community information, a special community information file is probably required. The Detroit Public Library's community information program (TIP) maintains its own pamphlet file designed to complement and supplement TIP's large directory-type community information database. Included in the file is information that cannot be logically entered into the larger database because of the format or extensive nature of the information provided. Much of this material is in printed form published by various governments and institutions.

Selection Tools

Material for a school library media center's community information file will be selected according to the general selection policy of the center, and selection of items reflects the overall missions and goals of the collection development plan. Sources for these materials are numerous, but they can also be illusive. For example, information on AIDS and HIV are often produced or available locally, but their availability and avenues of distribution may not include school media centers. The same is true of other special service groups. Often the availability of such materials are listed or reviewed in little known, specialized newsletters and announcements. The school library media specialist is best advised to develop contacts with authorities in areas of interest and request that they be placed on mailing lists. Routine contact with websites may also be used to identify materials, as often publications are announced and listed on special-interest websites.

Review and enumeration sources useful for selection include the periodical *VOYA: Voice of Youth Advocates* (http://www.voya.com), H. W. Wilson's *The Vertical File* (http://www.hwwilson.com/print/vfi.html), Online Computer Library Center's (OCLC) *Public Affairs Information Service* (http://www.pais.org), lists produced by the U.S. Government Printing Office (GPO) (http://www.access.gpo.gov), state government publication lists, and other sources. Materials may also be copied (following copyright provisions) from local sources, such as newspapers, newsletters, and magazines.

Acquisition of Materials

These materials are acquired in several ways. Requests using telephone, fax, e-mail, or mail requests are appropriate. A standard bibliographic form needs to be maintained whereby all information regarding the request is recorded. See Figure 3.3 for a suggested form.

Community Information File Acquisition Form

Bibliographic Information:

Author _____
Title _____
Publisher _____ Date _____
ISBN _____ Cost _____
Address of source _____
Phone/Fax/Email contacts _____
Date of request and/or Receipt_____
Source of review/citation _____
Subjects _____
Requested and/or Recommended by _____

Notes:

Figure 3.3 Community Information File Acquisition Form

For programs that wish to collect at a comprehensive level, commercial clipping sources and companies that acquire pamphlets and other materials on a subscription basis are available (http://www.internetprguide.com/clipping_services).

Management of the File

The information file must to be managed well. Weeding or "deselecting" items in the file as they become dated is paramount to its success as a community information tool. Current materials or replacement materials on topics must be acquired in a systematic way as needed. Some of the materials in the file have historical value and must be kept and organized so that they are accessible within their historical context. Clara L. Sitter addresses many of these management problems in a practical way in her 1992 book on the information file and is well worth consulting.[23]

THE PICTURE, VIDEO, AND AUDIO COLLECTIONS

Curriculum and Instructional Uses

Curriculum and instructional approaches have influenced the use of the picture file for decades. Its use as a community information file is important because it can center on community images. These images can be of value to inform about community, but the picture file's support of curriculum and instruction remains its most useful feature. Items in the picture file can consist of art reproductions, clippings from print sources, and original photoprints. The pictures in the file need to be appropriately mounted and stored. In a well-maintained file, pictures are indexed according to a subject headings list that reflects the needs for instruction and curriculum support. Historical items within the picture file may require more specialized subject headings.

New Technologies

Advances in technology have introduced new ways of offering pictures. For example, the 35mm camera permitted the introduction of slide collections, and the computer has added to this array of visuals by allowing for digitized imagery. Picture collections focusing on community information can include digitized pictures of historical buildings, personalities, street scenes, local events, architectural features, and other aspects from the local environment.

Resources

The school library media specialist can locate pictorial materials through various sources. Art slides are often acquired from commercial sources, and high-quality pictures are available for purchase from many sources. The library staff can also take their cameras into the community and take their own pictures of local features and events. Websites offer picture collections as well. Copyright and permission regulations must be well understood in terms of what can be copied and how it can be copied for permanent storage and use. The taking of pictures of sites and individuals must also follow institutional guidelines and legal requirements. Release forms asking permission to take pictures should be a part of acquisition policy.

Over the years, recording technologies had made possible the production of sound recordings in various formats (phonodisks and audiotapes). Again, following copyright considerations, school library media centers can collect recordings of local interests, including musical programs, talks and addresses, and local events. Some commercial television and radio stations may release recordings of their broadcasts for inclusion in a community information collection. School library media centers can also collect and develop oral history collections that include interviews with citizens about various aspects of community history.

Collecting video and audio recordings are similar. Video and audio recording technologies enhance the power of pictures by adding sound and movement to pictures. Much of the collection principles regarding the development and maintenance of the picture file are applicable to a video and audio collection.

COMMUNITY INFORMATION BULLETIN BOARDS

Resources

Closely related to the information file is the community information bulletin board. This relationship between the two is evident because of the nature of information and in the predominance of print format that this information generally takes. The pamphlet file is often not readily visible to the public, and much of the information will be overlooked if not displayed in a unique way. The Detroit Public Library's TIP service actually considers the two as one and the same. Likewise, Brake, in his model for community information in the school libraries, recommended that a community bulletin board be provided.

Items that are posted include community events notices (e.g., musical and drama productions, concerts, and fairs) and government regulations or requirements (e.g., military registrations, notifications about immigration requirement). Computer URL addresses to local information can also be posted.

Retention and Uses

Once these notices become dated, they can be removed and destroyed or placed in the pamphlet file if they have informational value going beyond current information needs. Some events might have historical or cultural value useful for future reference. For example, announcements of school band concerts might be filed as follows:

JONES HIGH SCHOOL BAND CONCERTS (A–Z)

or

JONES HIGH SCHOOL EVENTS (BAND CONCERTS) A–Z

The community bulletin board is an important access point for community information as with all other access provisions; the design and presentation of the community bulletin board must be carefully considered. Chapter 5 discusses some of the important details of how to design and present community bulletin boards.

SCHOOL ARCHIVES

In terms of community information, the school library media center may take responsibility for some aspects of a school's archives. Certain types of materials, such as school yearbooks, are generally expected to be found in the center's collection. The community information aspect of archives comes into play with the decision to collect in certain areas of school activities. For example, who systematically collects and preserves for the school such items as announcements and news releases, newspaper articles, biographical features appearing in the local press, video or audio productions of personalities and events, drama, music, and athletic programs? Even small schools have extensive social and cultural lives, producing a great deal of materials and documents. The school library media center may elect to comprehensively collect this material, or it may decide to collect in only certain areas. Not everything produced by the school needs to be collected and preserved. Archivists suggest that items and groups of items be assessed first for their historical and cultural value before they become a part of an archival collection.[24] Organization of a school archives needs to follow general principles of archival management. Standard archival organization requires that materials be organized according to the provenance or units of an organization that produced the materials.[25]

Another approach is to have archival materials integrated into the local information file with appropriate subject headings applied. The problem with this approach is that archival materials often require special handling and storage, and their housings in the vertical file may compromise these items over time.

REFERENCE AND GIVEAWAY MATERIALS

Reference materials and giveaway materials are important in all community information collections. Brake suggested that the collecting and making accessible of local directories and guides produced in the casement of the school are necessary for a school library media center community information program. Internet provides a considerable amount of local directory information, but it is often hard to access. To help alleviate this access problem, the center's staff can create a printed guide or directory to websites and other Internet references relating to local organizations and affairs and display this along with other directories.

Brake also suggested that free giveaway materials become a part of the school library media center's community information services. The Detroit Public Library's TIP program also provides giveaway items. In schools, many departments and services have access to free materials and are eager to distribute them widely. To sustain such a program, the school library media specialist can work in cooperation with the administration, the school counselor's office, the school nurse, food services, and others to see that materials are acquired and distributed in accordance with school policy, including the school materials selection policy. The types of free giveaway materials are extensive and can include election registration information, driver's license information and instruction booklets, diet and health information, community mental health pamphlets, employment and job support information, and information about recreational entertainment events.[26] In a community that has a large immigrant population, libraries should provide information on citizenship classes, information about social security cards, children's health services, and other family-based needs.

PROVIDING ACCESS TO COMMUNITY INFORMATION

Management of a community information service requires that policies and routines regarding cataloging and organization of materials be developed. There are many approaches to materials organization that have been taken over the years that are applicable to community information. More details on organizational approaches are discussed in chapter 5, but a brief overview will be given here.

The earliest means of access was to have community information listed on three-by-five-inch index cards or a typed list maintained as a separate file. Another approach that soon followed was to have the directory information integrated into the public card catalog. These catalog cards followed a uniform record form, as given in Figure 3.4. The online catalog widely introduced in the 1990s now allows records describing community information to be created and added directly to the catalog alongside other information held by a library. This procedure was facilitated by the development of a MARC format for community information. Figure 3.5, an example from the Public Libraries of Saginaw Michigan online catalog (http://webpac.vlc.lib.mi.us/Saginaw.html), shows catalog records created using the MARC format.

Central Texas Lyric Opera (Austin) [organization resource] /
Albert Smith, Public Information Officer. – Opera Square (111 Barton Springs Road, 99999) : 555-5555, 9 a.m.-5 p.m.

Audience level: 7th-12th grade.
Summary: The Opera will provide information on opera productions and performance. Guided tours of facilities are available upon request. Tours of facilities include rehearsal halls, recording studio, costume and set construction shops. Requests for tours must be made 48 hours ahead. Free, scheduled lectures and recitals are available as announced. The Opera also operates a school for qualified students. Admission is by audition only and tuition cost vary depending on ability to pay. Scholarship support is available by application.

1. Cultural Organizations. 2. Music. 3. Music Education. 4. Music Organizations. 5. Opera. I. Smith, Albert.

Based on AACR2 rules as suggested by Doris H. Clack, and cited in *The Collection Program in Schools*, by Phyllis J. Van Orden, 3rd.ed., p. 65-66.

Figure 3.4 Community Information Catalog Record

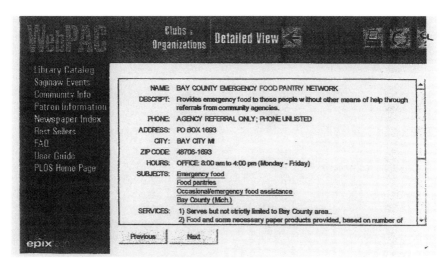

Figure 3.5 Public Libraries of Saginaw Catalog Record. Used by permission of the Public Libraries of Saginaw.

With the introduction of the Internet and web pages, some libraries have added community information as links to their own web page structure. Figure 3.6, the Austin weblink "Everything Austin, Texas," was created by the Austin History Center for the Austin Public Library (http://www.ci.austin.tx.us/library/ea_index.htm).

This avenue of linking to community information seems a viable approach for school library media center, and some school systems' web pages offer links to community information. The Baltimore (Maryland) County Public Schools, through its Office of Library Information Services, offers links to the public library catalog as well as to a community information network in the area (http://www.bcps.org/offices/).

The Internet also provides links to lists of individual school library media centers that maintain websites. These sites offer examples of how to design and create web pages. For more detailed information, consult such sites as "School Libraries on the Web," available at http://www.sldirectory.com, and "Planning a Web Page for Your Library?", available at http://www.oklibs.org/oaslms/news/librarywebs.htm. In addition to directories, the Internet offers sources for instruction on how the school media specialists can prepare web pages. See "Helps for Creating Your Own School Library Web Page," available at http://www.lili.org/education/create.htm.

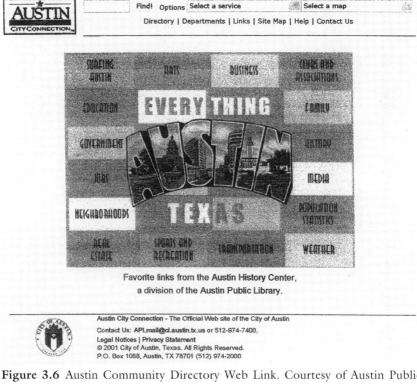

Favorite links from the **Austin History Center**,
a division of the **Austin Public Library**.

Figure 3.6 Austin Community Directory Web Link. Courtesy of Austin Public Library.

SUBJECT APPROACHES TO COMMUNITY INFORMATION

Management of the various files just discussed requires consideration of subject access. The following is a brief overview of some of the approaches that are available to the school library media specialist as he or she considers access options.

The Community Information Directory and Pamphlet File

As discussed previously, major subject headings lists, such as *Sears*, the Newark list, and the Toronto Public Libraries lists, have provided structures for community information based on geographic headings. Under such geographic headings, appropriate community information headings offer access:

Newark List (Miriam Ball, ed.)
- **N. J. Unemployment. Relief Measures**
- **N. J. Vocational Education**
- **Essex Co. Elections. Registration**
- **Essex Co. Rent**
- **Newark. Art Associations**

Sears List (Joseph Mill, ed.)
- **Chicago (Ill.)—Descriptions—Views**
- **Chicago. (Ill.)—Directories**

Toronto List
- **Canada—Science Council**
- **Toronto—Districts**
- **Toronto—Festivals**

Joanna F. Fountain recommends a number of headings that can be used to access local information, including these:[27]

Name of City [e.g., **Boston**]
— **Metropolitan Area**
— **Region**
— **Suburban Area**

Name of Rivers [e.g., **Red River**]
— **Region**
— **Valley**

Name of Geographic Features [e.g., **Balcones Fault Line, Austin, Texas**]
Regions [e.g., **Appalachian Region**]

These subject headings are designed to reflect the goals of traditional libraries' access needs and have been developed with that rationale in mind. The older lists also reflect the time periods in which they were created. On the whole, these lists do not address human service needs as specifically as may be needed in some community information programs. The human service needs influenced the community information directory and the pamphlet file of the Detroit Public Library's TIP program to move to a human service topology approach. As mentioned previously, TIP adopted *A Taxonomy of Human Services*.[28] This topology has several levels of entry as it moves from the general to the specific. Indexers can select terms at any level. Margaret Bruni, in her discussion of how TIP uses the list, provides these examples for employment and income:[29]

Level I   **Income Security**
Level II   **Employment**

Level III   **Employment Preparation**
Level IV   **Job Training**
Level V   **On-the-Job Training**

The Picture/Graphics File

Access to picture images has been considered by many, including museums, archives, film libraries, and school library media centers. Libraries, archives, and museums, as discussed in this chapter, have focused largely on the value of pictures to instruction and curriculum and on the information they provide about the community. Among others, Donna Hill offered these curriculum-support examples in her book on managing the picture file:

COMMUNITY LIFE
RIVERS AND STREAMS
ROADS AND STREETS[30]

Within these subject categories, individual rivers, roads, streets, and so on, can be filed alphabetically by name, **RIVERS AND STREAMS. COLORADO RIVER (TEXAS)**. Karen Gilbert also suggests that pictures can be accessed by locality subject designations. These can include specific buildings (e.g., banks, churches, tabernacles, shopping malls). Included here are other pictures that can be identified by locality[31] (e.g., **FIRST METHODIST CHURCH, AUSTIN, TEXAS**). Further discussion concerning the organization of pictures and graphic items is found in chapter 5.

The School Archives

As discussed previously, archives are customarily arranged by the unit within an organization that produced the items and by record groups. This can be an administrative office, such as the principal's office, or an academic department. A record group is a grouping of records that reflect certain characteristics. It is generally used to designate a unit or the dates when the records were produced. The following example is based on materials first being organized around a record group produced by an academic department—the school band.

In this example, a provenance arrangement (the group that created the documents—the Band) maintains original order of creation and a record group keeps related records together:

Record Group 1 (RG 1)
JOHNSON HIGH SCHOOL. BAND.
Contests and Awards, 1960–1980
Phonodisk Recordings, 1960–1980
Public Concert Programs, 1960–1980.

The provenance arrangement can be as simple or as detailed as needed. A simpler approach might be this: **JOHNSON HIGH SCHOOL. BAND (1960–1980)** with items filed alphabetically by subject.

CHALLENGES TO MATERIALS

Community information is judged according to standards as outlined in the school's materials selection policy and, like all other judicially elected materials, must be protected from censorship. Perhaps because community information is so closely involved with the life of the community, certain problems can be anticipated, such as dogmatic religious information, political organizations that support candidates, organizations that have membership restrictions, and groups that advocate for issues and government policies. A well-thought-out selection policy can offer guidance regarding these areas. Complaints may come because of omissions, inclusion of inaccurate or out-of-date materials, or the perceived inappropriateness of content. Complaints about the omission or lack of coverage of subjects are easily addressed. After reviewing the nature of the complaint regarding omission or lack of subject coverage, if the staff feels the complaint is justified, steps can be taken to acquire needed materials.

Content complaints regarding materials are treated differently. Following generally accepted procedures, such complaints must be documented. The complainant should be asked to give a written, signed statement outlining the nature of the complaint (a form can be provided). The complaint form should outline the procedures that will be followed once the complaint is formally filed. The complainant should be told that no action can be taken unless a formal, written complaint is on file. Upon receipt of the formal complaint, it is appropriately acknowledged. From there, the complaint is considered as any other materials complaint. Based on school policy and procedures, this includes reviews and possibly appeals at the local school and school district levels. Final authority rests with the school district's governing board. In the United States, as well as elsewhere, the board should understand that if it decides to remove materials, it must do so in accordance with law and court rulings. In the United States, students' First Amendment rights and their right to information must be considered.

The American Library Association (www.ala.org) and other professional and civil rights groups, such as the American Civil Liberties Union (ACLU) (http://www.aclu.org), as well as organizations in other countries (http://hrd-euromaster.venis.it/links/09.htm), offer guidance on how to protect freedom of access to information in accordance with prevailing governmental constitutions, policies, and court rulings.

CONCLUSION

Community information is vital if a holistic school media center information program is to be maintained. As long ago as the 1940s and 1950s, authorities such as Louis Shores and Margaret Rufsvold stated that community information was a part of library services and collection development. In the 1980s, Shirley Fitzgibbons identified community information as one of the six major aspects of information services.[32] Until now, most of the enthusiasm, models, and experiences for providing community information have come from public libraries. Today, school library media programs have the opportunity to take these experiences and mold them to fit their own unique requirements. Community information can play an important role in meeting the information and personal needs of students, supporting instruction and curriculum, and promoting information literacy and critical thinking skills.

NOTES

1. Ken Haycock, ed., *Foundations of Effective School Library Media Programs* (Englewood, Colo.: Libraries Unlimited, 1999).

2. Phyllis J. Van Orden and Kay Bishop, *The Collection Program in Schools: Concepts, Practices and Information Sources*, 3rd ed. (Englewood, Colo.: Libraries Unlimited, 2001).

3. Blanche Woolls, *The School Library Media Manager*, 2nd ed. (Englewood, Colo.: Libraries Unlimited, 1999).

4. W. Bernard Lukenbill, *Collection Development for a New Century in the School Library Media Center* (Westport, Conn.: Greenwood Press, 2002), 17–18.

5. Robert D. Stueart and Barbara B. Moran, *Library and Information Center Management*, 5th ed. (Littleton, Colo.: Libraries Unlimited, 1998), 31–86.

6. Lukenbill, 19, citing Stueart and Moran, 29.

7. Dick Manikowski, "Setting Inclusion/Exclusion Criteria: Determining the Scope of a Resource File," *Information and Referral* 17 (1995): 1–22.

8. American Library Association, *Guidelines for Establishing Community Information and Referral Services in Public Libraries; With a Selectively Annotated Guide to the Literature of Information and Referral*, ed. Norman L. Mass and Dick Manikowski, 4th ed. (Chicago: ALA, 1997), 11.

9. Manikowski, 1.

10. Ibid., 2.

11. Ibid., 3, 7–8.

12. Ibid., 5.

13. Terence Brake, *The Need to Know: Teaching the Importance of Information.* Final Report for the Period January 1978–March 1979. (London: The British Library, 1980), 9.

14. Manikowski, 6–10.

15. Lukenbill, 49–66, 76–80.

16. Robert Croneberger and Carolyn Luck, "Analyzing Community Human Information Needs: A Case Study," *Library Trends* 24 (January 1976): 515–25.

17. Toronto Public Libraries, *Subject Headings for Vertical Files*, 2nd ed. (Toronto: The Libraries, 1971).

18. Minnie Earl Sears, *Sears List of Subject Headings*, 17th ed., ed. Joseph Miller (New York: H. W. Wilson Co., 2000).

19. Hennepin County Library, *[HCL] Catalog Bulletin* (Edina, Minn.: The Library, 1973, 1999).

20. Ibid., *Cumulative Authority List* (Minnetonka, Minn.: The Library, August 5, ca. 1979, 1993).

21. *A Taxonomy of Human Services: A Conceptual Framework with Standard Terminology and Definitions for the Field*, 3rd ed. (Los Angeles: AIRS and Info Line of Los Angeles, 1994). *Supplement*, 1998 [Electronic format updates available on subscription basis after 1998].

22. Margaret Gillis Bruni, "Indexing with the AIRS/Info Line Taxonomy of Human Services," *Information and Referral* 17 (1995): 43.

23. Clara L. Sitter, *The Vertical File and Its Alternatives: A Handbook* (Englewood, Colo.: Libraries Unlimited, 1992).

24. Elizabeth Yakel, *Starting an Archives* (Metuchen, N.J.: Society of American Archivists and Scarecrow Press, 1994), 1.

25. Heartsill Young, ed., *The ALA Glossary of Library and Information Science* (Chicago: American Library Association, 1983), 181.

26. Gayle S. Lucas, "Maintaining a Pamphlet File to Supplement the Traditional I&R Resource File," *Information and Referral* 17 (1995): 73–84.

27. Joanna F. Fountain, *Subject Headings for School and Public Libraries: An LCSH/Sears Companion*, 2nd ed. (Englewood, Colo.: Libraries Unlimited, 1996), xii.

28. See note 21.

29. Bruni, 44.

30. Donna Hill, The *Picture File: A Manual and a Curriculum-Related Subject Heading List*, 2nd ed. (Hamden, Conn.: Linnet Books, 1978).

31. Karen Diane Gilbert, *Picture Indexing for Local History Materials* (Monroe, N.Y.: Library Research Associates, 1973).

32. Shirley A. Fitzgibbons, "Reference and Information Services for Children and Young Adults: Definitions, Services, and Issues," *The Reference Librarian* 7/8 (Spring/Summer 1983): 1–30.

CHAPTER 4

Networking: The Heart of Community Information

INTRODUCTION

In this chapter we will consider how to use networking in the development of a school-based community information program. Because of the limited history of community information in schools, this discussion will rely heavily on public library experiences. This chapter will attempt to explain how to develop an effective network system bringing the school library media center into contact with the wider community. Major points of reference will include definitions of networking; networking experiences in the library community, including school library media center experiences; building community resources through networking; referrals and referral strategies; theories about community and individual identity development; and an evaluation procedure designed to assess program impact.

NETWORKS AND NETWORKING

Network is an old word. First introduced into English in 1560, lexicographers defined it as a "fabric or structure of cords or wires that cross at regular intervals and are knotted or secured at the crossing." That definition has both practical and philosophical meaning for us today. In 1940, *networking* was incorporated into American English and provides us with our modern understanding of a system of communication. The 1940 meaning defines the word as "the exchange of information or services among individuals, groups, or institutions." Later, with the widespread use of computers, networking became closely associated with the process of joining computers together in a united pattern for the transmission of data.[1]

NETWORKS IN COMMUNITY LIFE

As we consider networks and networking from a school library media center perspective, we must consider several aspects of networks and networking. Regardless of where it is located, a community information system cannot function effectively without some association with networks.

One of the most influential forms of networks to affect the school library media center is bibliographic and informational utilities such as OCLC (Online Computer Library Center) (http://www.oclc.org/home). Local and state networks similar to the former Texas Library Connection (TLC) and the Harrington Library Consortium (HLC) in Texas have likewise directly influenced the overall effectiveness of school library media center management and the delivery of information resources (www.hlc-lib.org/index.html). For example, the HLC offers links to Internet resources for youth, such as "Ben's Guide to U. S. Government for Kids" (http://bensguide.gpo.gov) and "WTAMU Free Databases Page" (www.wtamu.edu/library/instruction/tplsdb.shtml). In addition to bibliographic records, while it existed, TLC provided subscription services to information systems such as the Gale Group and the Britannica Online School Edition. Often, members of individual school communities (teachers, parents, and students) had access to these sources from their homes. Unfortunately, TLC was not funded for continuation by the 2003 Texas legislature.

Community information and I&R networks that exist in the local environment are important in developing a school library media center community information service. These systems offer electronic links to important resources in the community. They are also sources of print and audiovisual materials.

Local as well as national I&R services and networks exist in a variety of contexts and serve a variety of information needs and client groups. As stated previously, selecting and linking to these networks must follow established materials selection policies and guidelines. Title XX of the Social Security Act of 1974 stated that I&R services were not for the poor alone. This government policy helped open I&R up to a wider contingency group. Consequently, I&R organizations serve an array of interests and are funded or operated by a variety of community and private groups and government units, including the United Way, public libraries, and public health departments.[2]

Stephen T. Bajjaly, associate professor, College of Library and Information Science at the University of South Carolina and founder of MidNet (www.midnet.sc.edu), writes extensively about the role of community networks and public libraries. In his research, Bajjaly identified 215 established community networks in the United States and Canada. However, less than one-third of these identified the library as a major partner.[3]

Local community network systems are based on usable computer technology that brings local information to citizens and encourages citizens to participate.[4] They also provide an effective means for local institutions, including schools, to collaborate on delivering local information.[5] Bajjaly outlines several important aspects of local community networks, all of which help to focus a community information program in the school library media center. Among these are equity of accessibility, decentralization of information (information available in variety of locations), and collaboration. Collaboration ensures that accurate answers are delivered from a variety of sources. He advises that information be gathered from a variety of sources, including cultural events; businesses; community organizations; educational and governmental agencies; health providers; public, special, and university libraries; media and news sources; sports and recreation; transportation; and weather.[6] For example, MidNet community information network offers many links to community information in the South Carolina midlands, including an interesting site on animals (http://www.midnet.sc.edu/animal) that provides a list of local laws concerning the care and owning of animals. The "Young Adults" link connects the user to schools and library resources in the area (www.midnet.sc.edu/ya/local.html). Figiures 4.1 and 4.2 show these resources.

Although many local community information networks have been created with little or no library connections, Bajjaly mentions several that have developed with library help and participation. Three Rivers Free-Net, sponsored by Pittsburgh's Carnegie Library (to be terminated by the library), and Austin Free-Net in Austin, Texas, are among these (http://trfn.clpgh.org and www.austinfree.net/afnhome.html). (See Figure 4.3.)

Local I&R services and networks in communities should also be considered for inclusion in the school library media centers. Some of these are special in terms of client groups served and interests covered. Because of the differences in the way I&R services are organized in communities, some of these may be difficult to locate. Levinson identified five kinds of I&R services. These include (1) clearinghouse informational I&R services that provide information and assistance to all inquiries; (2) freestanding I&R systems that are generic services that operate independently and provide services to the general public; (3) intra-agency I&R services that are sponsored and supported by an agency such as a public library; (4) decentralized I&R networks that bring together several separate I&R services in a given area or

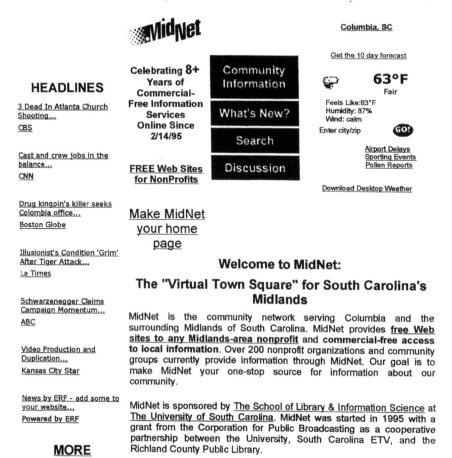

Figure 4.1 MidNet Home Page. Used by permission of MidNet.

organizational structure, such as military installations; and (5) centralized I&R networks that include multiple I&R services accountable to a single I&R agency or regional authority.[7] Directories of many I&R services are available on the web. For example, Community Information & Referral located in Phoenix, Arizona, offers a national directory of many local and state I&R services that fall into many of these categories (http://www.cirs.org/outside.html).

Nevertheless, some of the most interesting or useful subject areas or local services may not be listed in such directories, thus requiring searches of local print directories and Internet sources. For example, organizations serving gay, lesbian, bisexual, and transgendered youth are not numerous, but access to them is often essential. "Out Youth Austin" is such an example.

Restricted: Young Adults Only!

The Chosen Ones

What's this about?

Click on any of the subject buttons below to link to lots and lots of web pages that ar always germane, sometimes fun, and sometimes almost awesome.

The 🔶 beside links within the subject areas below signifies local South Carolina or Midlands information.

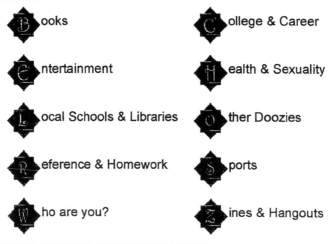

🔶ooks 🔶ollege & Career

🔶ntertainment 🔶ealth & Sexuality

🔶ocal Schools & Libraries 🔶ther Doozies

🔶eference & Homework 🔶ports

🔶ho are you? 🔶ines & Hangouts

Hotlines for Teen Help

National Runaway Switchboard
   You can get help 24 hours a day, 365 days a year. Contact NRS, 1-800-621-4000, if you nee
   for yourself or a friend.

Teenline
   1-800-922-2283 or 1-843-744-HELP
   Free and confidential listening and help for teens in Berkeley, Dorchester and Charleston Co
   Sponsored by Trident United Way.

Youth Crisis Hotline 800-448-4663

Figure 4.2 MidNet Young Adult Link Page. Used by permission of MidNet.

Their web page offers information about the local organization as well as national resources (www.outyouth.org). "Teens @ MPL," designed by the Marion Public Library in Ohio, is a site designed to reflect the needs and interest of teenagers and offers links to many kinds of national informational

CARNEGIE LIBRARY OF PITTSBURGH

THREE RIVERS

FREE-NET
PITTSBURGH, PA

The Three Rivers Free-Net, part of the Carnegie Library of Pittsburgh since
TRFN's inception in 1992, has moved its Subject Guide to the Library's
website so that it can be combined with the Library's resources. This will
result in a more comprehensive and more accessible directory of web
resources that can better serve the needs of Pittsburgh and Southwestern
Pennsylvania.

Search the Internet	Resource Guide	Pittsburgh Organizations
Events	Discover Pittsburgh!	News / Sports / Weather
TRFN Organizations	About TRFN	Search TRFN

4400 Forbes Avenue, Pittsburgh, PA 15213-4080
Phone: 412-622-8862; FAX: 412-688-8609
E-Mail: trfn@trfn.clpgh.org
Last modified : *Thursday, 12-Dec-2002 11:52:04
EST.*
Copyright (c) 1996-2002, Three Rivers Free-Net,
Carnegie Library of Pittsburgh. All Rights
Reserved.
Disclaimer

*Major Funding for Carnegie Library of Pittsburgh
is provided by The Allegheny Regional Asset
District*

Figure 4.3 Three Rivers Free-Net. Used by permission of Carnegie Library of
Pittsburgh.

resources (http://www.marion.lib.oh.us/Teens/teensinfo.htm). (See Figures
4.4 and 4.5).

Local hotlines and crisis centers are additional services that must be considered. Most communities of any size offer such support services. A simple
Internet search using as a search term "hotlines" or "crisis centers," together
with the name of a specific geographic area, can generally retrieve useful
directory information.

META-NETWORKING AND COMMUNITY
INFORMATION

Sociologists now use the term *meta-networking* to refer to the complex
world of community. Meta-networking ushers in an important role for all
professionals, including school library media specialists, as it involves helping communities form positive support systems. Formal and informal net-

Welcome to

About Us ⊠

Special Events ⊠

Programs ⊠

Calendar ⊠

How to Help ⊠

Resources ⊠

Contacts ⊠

Scrapbook ⊠

Job Openings ⊠

Out Youth is a non-profit organization providing support and services to gay, lesbian, bisexual, transgender, and questioning youth ages 12 to 19 in Austin and Central Texas. We offer peer support groups, counseling, educational programs, social activities and community outreach. Mostly, we are a safe place to fearlessly be yourself and we are working to make our community just as safe for GLBTQ youth!

Please visit our <u>special events</u> page for information about the upcoming <u>Laugh Out Proud!</u>

Now you can support Out Youth by donating online... Just click the button below to donate through Pay Pal or visit our <u>"How to Help" page</u> to find out more about how you can help us work toward making Central Texas safe for all youth.

Figure 4.4 Out Youth Austin Home Page. Used by permission of Out Youth Austin.

working within a community helps the community define itself and influences how it will behave as a collective unit. Well-connected communities exist when people come together, bringing with them the power of both diversity and interlocking relationships. Positive interpersonal networks support familiar and supportive patterns of interaction and contribute to volunteerism and the infrastructures needed for vibrant community life. Professionals have the responsibility to help create opportunities that support ways of connecting and communication across the many divisions in a community, including race, class, gender, nationality, culture, business, and religion.[8]

The school recognizes community and the promotion of community life as one of its missions.[9] In recent times, the connection between school and community has become even more pressing because of a world that many perceive to be at the edge of chaos. School library media specialists can use community information services to promote community and lessen the hardships of living in a complex society.

The building of a structure that can support a school library media center community information service begins at home. A wise approach is to identify sources in and around the library media center that can contribute

Hotlines & Information

HOTLINES

Alateen/Alanon	800-356-9996
Mothers Against Drunk Driving (MADD)	800-438-MADD
Boys Town	800-448-3000
Child Help USA	800-422-4453
National Domestic Violence Hotline	800-799-7233
National Clearinghouse of Child Abuse & Neglect	800-394-3366
Rape, Abuse & Incest National Network	800-656-4673
National Runaway Switchboard	800-621-4000
National Referral Network for Kids in Crisis	800-KID-SAVE
National AIDS Hotline	800-342-AIDS
STD National Hotline	800-227-8922

Alcohol, Drugs & Tobacco | Babysitting | Body Image, Eating Disorders, Nutrition & Exercise
Education | Environmental & Animal Groups | Health
Leadership Programs | Self-Help | Social Welfare Programs
Sports | Teen Dating & Sexuality | Teen Pregnancy & Parenting
Teen Violence & Safety | Teens Behind the Wheel | Volunteering

Alcohol, Drugs and Tobacco
Alcohol and Other Drug Information for Teens
Dance Safe
Drug Facts
The Truth.com

to top

Figure 4.5 Marion, Ohio, Public Library Young Adult Page. Used by permission of Marion Public Library.

to the resources that will enrich the collection. Consider these sources as ˌtal first contacts:

The School Community

- Student, teachers, support staff, administrators at both the building and district levels;
- Parents and parent leaders;
- Parents, teachers, and staff organizations.

Once the local school community has been canvassed, the collection can be enlarged by including the larger community. This larger community can be defined by interests and needs, by geography, or by social and cultural expectations.

The Larger Community

- Government agencies (local, district, state and provincial, national);
- Support services, such as hotlines and crisis centers;

- Information and referral centers and networks;
- Businesses;
- Profit and nonprofit organizations and clubs;
- Religious organizations and centers;
- Consultants, parishioners, and subject experts;
- Tradespeople;
- Interesting individuals, such as authors and inventors;
- Hobbyists and adventurers;
- Recreation and entertainment providers;
- Local mass media, such as television and radio;
- Other persons and groups that fall beyond clearly defined categories.

Contact people and organizations in an appropriate manner and inquire about the resources they might be able to provide. The school library media center staff (both professional and support staff) can do this in several ways: directly through conversations, person-to-person or telephone interviews, mailed questionnaires, and surveys. Chapter 3 provides a suggested assessment form for documenting and evaluating information for inclusion in a community information system. The following are some general assessment questions to include:

- For businesses, ask what their product is and assess its educational and interest value to students and to the school curriculum and community;
- For students and other individuals, ask what their interests are, where they go for fun, entertainment, and services. Ask whether they have hobbies or collections they would like to share. Ask if they have interesting travel or adventure stories to share.
- For government agencies, ask what their services are, what client groups they address, what geographical or administrative areas they serve.
- For clubs, organizations, and other service providers, such as religious groups, ask about their major interests and service areas. Ask how their resources can help students learn in accordance with the mission and curriculum of the school.

Figure 4.6 illustrates those important relationships.

The library media specialist must work at developing a support network of information providers and clusters. This means knowing the community well. The community must include both the school community and the community external to it. The Detroit Public Library (DPL) realized the importance of knowing the community in the early development of its community information service. One method it used was the "community walk," whereby the staff actually goes out into the community and makes direct contact with businesses, organizations, clubs, churches, and individuals who might offer vital community information resources. The principle here is that in order to maintain a vital community information service, the library media staff must contact and be involved in the life of the community. The community walk as used by DPL was both an informal community analysis

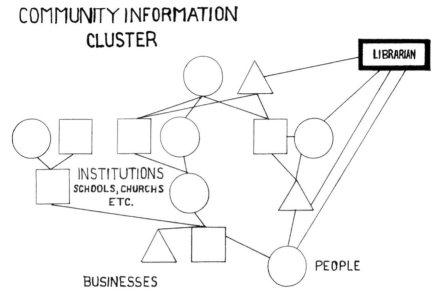

COMMUNITY INFORMATION CLUSTER

LIBRARIAN

INSTITUTIONS
SCHOOLS, CHURCHS
ETC.

PEOPLE

BUSINESSES

Figure 4.6 Community Cluster Diagram

method as well as a marketing device. The DPL used the walk to advertise the services of the library, to promote its new TIP community information program, and to discover needs and wants within the community. In targeting such entities as businesses, churches, bars, and gas stations, it not only promoted itself, it also discovered local resources, services, and contacts available in the community. The walk also prepared the library to meet the many differences in culture, social life, and group and individual expectations.[10]

School library media specialists can "walk" their communities as well. They can visit local establishments, and they can join appropriate clubs and organizations. They can also accomplish much by simply being in the community and making astute observations and contacts. Most people and groups are happy to contribute once they are contacted and realize that there is an interest in what they do and what they can offer the school community.

HELPFUL THEORIES AND CONCEPTS IN NETWORK AND COMMUNITY DEVELOPMENT

Theories and conceptual models help define practice and lend focus and understanding to everyday operations. Theoretical constructs, such as socio-cultural perspective, symbolic interactionism, symbolic functionalism, exchange theory, and community psychology, seem especially useful in helping to underscore the importance of a school library media center's role in community development and networking through the provision of community information.[11]

Briefly stated, *sociocultural perspective theory* maintains that children learn to be who they are and learn about their role in culture and society by maintaining a cooperative dialogue with more knowledgeable and informed members of their culture and society. *Symbolic interactionism* is concerned with observing and explaining the symbols and information used by people as they interact with one another. *Symbolic functionalism* states that a social system is made up of parts, and each part contributes to the functioning of the whole system. *Ethnomethodological theory* contends that people create social structures through their actions and interactions. In so doing, they continually create their realities in an attempt to make sense out of the life they experience. *Exchange theory*, encountered in both business and not-for-profit organizations, holds that everything has a price. All individuals and groups calculate the costs and benefits of their actions and services, and often it is necessary to exchange services and goods with others in order to derive needed benefits.

Although the theories mentioned are useful in concept development, community psychology seems especially appropriate in this discussion and perhaps deserves a bit more attention. Community psychology is an application theory that seeks to influence and advance society through improving the behavior of people in institutions and organizations as they interact and function in society. Social observers Murrary Levine and David Perkins consider community psychology as a preventative approach to social problems, and they place it within an ecological context. They view human behavior as how a person uses and adapts to resources and circumstances available in life. The community psychology model allows for the introduction of resources as an intervention strategy by community institutions whenever problems are discovered in the ecological systems. New services and better social networks are created or improved with the goal of bringing about positive change through resource use by both individuals and communities.[12] Educators Patrick Penland and James Williams suggest that libraries are applying principles of community psychology when they coordinate and disseminate information based on community interests and needs. According to Penland and Williams, librarians are involved in community psychology when they "promote the maximum exchange of verbal, nonverbal, visual, and written information with the community."[13] When applying community psychology principles, librarians rely on the mass media for information about and from the community; they understand the educational experiences of members of the community, they provide consultative services regarding information needs, and they provide retrieval access to information. Community psychology in librarianship strongly implies that librarians become resource coordinators regarding information about and from the community.[14] Effective communication on the part of the librarian with the community is imperative if the community psychology model is to function.[15]

Curriculum and instructional theories also play important roles in a school library media center's community information design and function. Curriculum and instructional and cognitive theories help place the role of a school-based community information program within the goals, objectives, and functional framework of student learning. These ideas are considered in more detail in chapter 2.

Most, if not all, of these theories and concepts underscore the important role that community information plays in the lives of students as they move into society as well-informed and capable people. At the application level, these theories are also helpful in justifying the social and educational role of a school library media center community information service.

PROGRAM IMPACT ASSESSMENT AND NETWORKING

In chapter 3 we discussed the need to evaluate community resources in terms of individual items. The discussion pointed out the importance of accuracy, age appropriateness, usefulness, and other criteria. Impact assessment is an evaluation procedure that can also play an important role in networking. It offers insight into how both communities and individuals react to programs and services, and how those programs and services advance positive community involvement.

Impact assessment is a process whereby the effects of a program or service are determined through a logical evaluation process designed to determine behavioral or attitudinal changes. The objective is to determine the positive influence that a program exerts on the behaviors, values, and attitudes of the clients or users of the program or service.

Impact assessment is challenging, but the United Way of America has developed guidelines for service programs based on impact assessment needs. With modifications, some of United Way's suggestions are applicable to school library media community information programs. The approach uses a system concept and categorizes the gathering of information into the following elements:

- Inputs: Resources dedicated to or consumed by the program;
- Activities: What the program does with the inputs to fulfill its mission;
- Outputs: The direct products of program activities; and
- Outcomes: Benefits for participants during and after program activities. (See Figure 4.7).[16]

Determinations of outcomes are based on several kinds of measurements that reflect the program's objectives and knowledge of participants and their

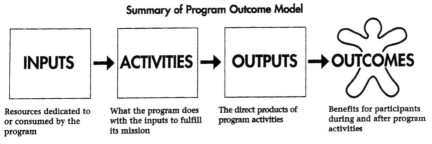

Summary of Program Outcome Model

INPUTS → ACTIVITIES → OUTPUTS → OUTCOMES

| Resources dedicated to or consumed by the program | What the program does with the inputs to fulfill its mission | The direct products of program activities | Benefits for participants during and after program activities |

Figure 4.7 United Way Model. Reprinted from *Measuring Program Outcomes: A Practical Approach* (1996). Used by permission, United Way of America.

social environment. Measurements can include observations, comments, and well-reasoned inferences.[17] Well-selected indicators also are necessary to measure impact outcomes. An indicator is information that will show how well the program is meeting the desired outcome. Indicators must be specific, observable, and measurable, and should present characteristics of change that will represent achievement of the program's outcomes. These characteristics must be stated in statistical terms, such as numbers and percentage, that can be easily calculated to summarize the degree of program achievement.[18]

Based on an I&R program example provided by United Way, a school library center community information program might look something like this:

- Outcome: Once informed of availability, users (students, teachers, parents) will access and use the library media center web page containing links to information sources within the local community.
- Indicators of this access and use:
  - ✔ Number and percent of observable hits to community information links;
  - ✔ Number and percent of teacher comments on how students use links for assignments;
  - ✔ Number and percent of student comments on how they use community resource links to fulfill assignments and for personal use;
  - ✔ Number and percent of teacher comments on how they use community links for instructional purposes;
  - ✔ Number and percent of parent comments on how their children use or mention having used community links suggested by the school library media center program;
  - ✔ Number and percent of user (students, teachers, parents, staff) comments on the appropriateness of links in terms of needs, subject content, and interest.[19]

Both participants and program characteristics may influence outcomes, and these can be used in the assessment of program effectiveness and may include age, sex, race, culture, educational levels and achievement, income of household, and level of family and individual functioning.

Outcome assessment relies on sources of data that are varied and rich. As indicated earlier, sources can include participants, teachers as both observers and participants, school records such as report cards, review of assignment grades and performance, program records and statistics such as questions asked, observations by staff of participant behaviors and attitudes, and recorded use of resources. Surveys and questionnaires may also be used to collect data.[20]

Figure 4.8, based on United Way's procedures, provides a framework of an outcomes measurement instrument.

Once the outcomes measurement forms have been administered, the data must be placed into formats that can provide statistics useful for analysis and narrative reporting. Figure 4.9, also based on United Way, offers this example.

Although these procedures are time-consuming, they are the best ways to show administrators and teachers that community information has value and impacts student learning. This approach not only improves accountability, it also offers valuable lessons in how to continually improve community information services and programs.

Worksheet 4

Outcome Measurement Framework

Program: _____

Outcome	Indicator(s) (may be more than one per outcome)	Data Source	Data Collection Method

Figure 4.8 United Way Outcome Measure Instrument. Reprinted from *Measuring Program Outcomes: A Practical Approach* (1996). Used by permission, United Way of America.

Comparative Findings for Two Youth Services Approaches: Team vs. Individual Activity Emphasis

(Data are for a one-year test; about 150 youth are included in each procedure.)

Approach Used	Percent of Youth Showing Increased Verbal Skills	Percent of Youth Showing Increased Interpersonal Skills
Team Activities	88%	46%
Individual Activities	92%	28%

Steps for Comparing Alternative Program Approaches

1. Identify the two practices or approaches to be compared. Perhaps one is an existing practice and the other is a new approach.

2. Choose a method for deciding which incoming youth will be served using which approach. The method should select a representative sample of the participants for each

Figure 4.9 United Way Statistical Report. United Way Statistical Measure Instruction. Reprinted from *Measuring Program Outcomes: A Practical Approach* (1996). Used by permission, United Way of America.

CONCLUSION

The development of a community information service in a school is challenging. It requires time, patience, and understanding of how complex systems are developed and maintained. It also requires an understanding of how modern communities acquire and use information. On a technical and human level, the school library media specialist must understand the important role that computer and human networks play in developing effective community information systems, and they must know how to become an effective player in networks. But above all, a sense of mission to improve the lives of students and their families (and the community at large) is at the heart of all good school-based community programs.

NOTES

1. *Webster's Ninth New Collegiate Dictionary* (Springfield, Mass.: Merriam-Webster, 1983), 794.

2. Risha W. Levinson, *New Routes to Human Services: Information and Referral* (New York: Springer, 2002), 27–28.

3. Stephen T. Bajjaly, *The Community Networking Handbook* (Chicago: American Library Association, 1999), xi.

4. Ibid., 1.

5. Ibid., 2.

6. Ibid., 6.

7. Levinson, 86.

8. Alison Gilchrist, "The Well-Connected Community: Networking to the 'Edge of Chaos.'" *Community Development Journal* 35 (July 2000): 264–75.

9. Carol Gestwicki, *Home, School, and Community Relations: A Guide to Working with Families,* 4th ed. (Albany, N.Y.: Delmar, 2000).

10. Robert Croneberger and Carolyn Luck, "Analyzing Community Human Information Needs: A Case Study," *Library Trends* 24 (January 1976): 518.

11. Jennifer Bothamley, ed., *Dictionary of Theories* (London: Gale Research International, 1993).

12. Murray Levine and David V. Perkins, *Principles of Community Psychology: Perspectives and Applications,* 2nd ed. (New York: Oxford University Press, 1997), 6.

13. Patrick R. Penland and James G. Williams, *Community Psychology and Coordination* (New York: Marcel Dekker), quote from cover statement.

14. Ibid., 5–12.

15. Ibid, 10–12.

16. United Way of America, *Measuring Program Outcomes: A Practical Approach,* written by consultants Harry Hatry and Therese van Houten, and by Margaret C. Planz and Martha Taylor Greenway of United Way of America (Alexandria, Va.: United Way of America, 1996), 3.

17. Ibid., 39.

18. Ibid., 61.

19. Ibid., 66.

20. Ibid., 90–93.

CHAPTER 5

Organizing the Collection: Technologies and Approaches

INTRODUCTION

This chapter introduces design factors to be considered and applied when packaging, marketing, and presenting community information to users. Major topics covered include the traditional vertical or information file, picture or graphic files, community information bulletin boards, the public online catalog (PAC) and how it can be used to provide community information, the computer as a tool for dissemination of community information, website construction and technologies, referral and advice-giving considerations, and archival organization.

PART 1. COMMUNICATION, CULTURE, AND DESIGN: CULTURAL AND SOCIAL FACTORS

The design and presentation of community information is a cultural and social communication process. As such, it involves the basic principles concerning the transmission of information within various social and cultural environments. In the context of the school library media center, this involves communication as a means of designing, marketing, packaging, organizing, and the overall presenting of information products to users of various backgrounds and experiences.

Cultural and social factors influence the selection of community information, including the informational nature of the content and its age appropriateness. Content appropriateness may be reflected both in the types of information presented as well as in narrative language. For example, depending on the content and audience, idiomatic and translation correctness are important considerations. Community information materials translated for Spanish-speaking students must be appropriate for the local population. Spanish language terms vary depending upon countries and regions, and local translations must be suited for the local user group. Some Spanish terms used in the Rio Grande Valley of Texas can differ in meaning and context from the same word or similar words used in Los Angeles.

Beyond that, in terms of community information, we must consider the importance and role that cultural values and expectations, or "cultural scripts," play in information dissemination. To generalize, but recognizing that individual differences exist, traditional American Hispanic cultures have much in common with other traditional cultures, and we can use some of the elements found there to emphasize the importance of understanding the mores of our communities as we plan and execute community information programs.

For example, in American Hispanic communities, family and family roles are powerful. Individuals identify strongly with family and family structure. This identification often extends beyond the immediate family into a large extended family and to family-accepted members of a community. Many Spanish populations place considerable importance on *simpatía*—harmony, positive social behavior, personal attractiveness, and frequent, positive social interactions. It is important to remember in terms of community information that, in this culture, it is more important to be valued than to do. In other words, information may not necessarily be used so much for doing something with it for personal gain as with sharing it as an enriching social contribution to family and friends. Because personal relationships are so important within this and other traditional cultures, the presentation of community information in terms of design and dissemination is extremely important.

In American Hispanic cultures, as well as with other cultural and religious groups, the significance given to the differences between male and female roles and family life is important to understand. Likewise, the role of authority, age, social class, and hierarchical relationships must be appreciated. Understanding "cultural scripts" and social interactions of all groups is paramount to the effective development of a community information program in the school.[1]

INFORMATION AND LEARNING DESIGN PRINCIPLES

Information presentation is not random. Information takes its meaning and value from the context in which it exists. This context directs and influences the design of information. Information is constructed to influence attitudes, beliefs, behavior, and values. At one end of the information continuum is governmental propaganda, such as that developed by Nazism (the National Socialist German Workers Party), constructed to mold the attitudes and behavior of a nation and social groups. At the other end is information developed to inform, with the purpose of encouraging and allowing for individual decisions and choices. Whatever the reason, information design and construction has many elements in common, all of which help people process information.

Psychological Perception

Perception as used in information processing is a complex process by which people receive and extract information from their various social and cultural environments. Perception is not absolute and varies from individual to individual and culture to culture. Perception helps people to extract and organize information. Research shows that people organize information around the following elements:

- Relationships
- Events
- Groupings
- Words
- Objects
- People

Nevertheless, selectivity influences how these organizational units are used. People attend to only a few of these units at a time, and this selectivity is precise in terms of the individual. Selectivity is based on familiarity, past experiences, interests, and needs. Information product designs need to provide reference points for the user so that individual perception can be related to the information.[2]

Perception has its limits. Most people cannot process all the information stimuli that come to them. Nevertheless, complex information can certainly be processed, but this is accomplished in incremental stages, reinforced by the time available to process the information. The information design must be well paced, short and uncluttered, and divided into small stages or categories. Information product designs need to provide reference points to help direct attention and increase retention of relevant information. For example, well-selected words and other verbal cues can help direct attention and increase perception of relevant information.[3]

Set

Set in information design is another important element because it establishes perimeters or boundaries and provides guidance for users. Set in

Figure 5.1 Set in Information Product Design

product design helps to direct users' expectations and influences their perception of the information. For example, set established by the information designer directs information processing by informing the user about coverage, defines the boundaries of information presentations, and directs the flow and direction of information presentation. A title caption for a community bulletin board is a set. Borders applied to information products, as provided in Figure 5.1, is another example of set.[4]

Repetition

The ability to remember information is influenced by how and how often it is encountered. In learning, the adage is that practice (repeating the concept) is necessary to learn the concept. In information product design, this generally means that a designer must plan to have relevant information repeated enough so that it is retained. Repetition in design can be accomplished through consistent use of the same or similar words, concepts, and ideas in interesting and slightly varying ways and arrangements. (See Figure 5.2).[5]

Learning Cues and Prompts

Learning cues and prompts are part of set in that they influence how the information is to be processed. Familiar learning cues include color and letter-

Figure 5.2 Repetition in information production design

ing, such as boldface fonts, italics, and underlining. Symbols, such as those used in music, sports, medicine, and other areas, are useful as learning cues and prompts. Directional markings such as arrows and bullets are also useful. (See Figure 5.3.)

The use of color that indicates meanings can be used as well. For example, yellow is often used for caution, while red is used to alert or warn of danger. Colors used to draw attention to a message and to set mood or tone are effective.[6] For example, red can suggest high emotions, while blues and greens offer calm and tranquility. On the other hand, designers need to be aware that some colors used in certain contexts will generate negative connotations. For example, pink and blue, suggesting male and female, might be viewed by some as sexist, while black, suggestive of evil, will certainly be viewed as racist.

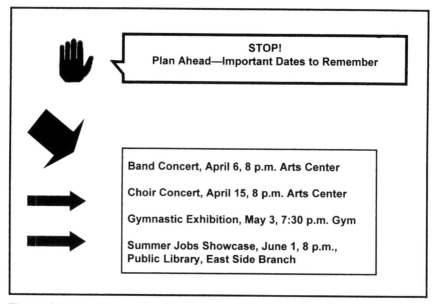

Figure 5.3 Learning Cues and Prompts in Information Product Design

Active Participation

Effect information designs invite the user to participate in meaningful ways. Questions and corrective feedback are excellent examples for promoting active participation. For example, community information bulletin boards can have captions that ask questions: "Need Something to Do This Week?— Try These . . ." Web designs can also do this by offering links and other options for making choices in how the information presented is processed at the individual level. "Frequently Asked Questions" is another form of activity participation.

Closure

All information messages need closure or a clearly marked ending. This can be a summary, a review, a concluding remark, or, on a website, a simple "return to home." A closure on a bulletin board can be a statement saying "For more information use the Community Information Computer Directory" or "More information is available from the librarian."[7]

CREATING DESIGNS

Many factors need to be considered when a specific design is created. Among these are format and structure, and design elements.

Format and Structure

Format is the structure on which a design is placed. Structure is, there-fore, the means by which the various elements in the design are placed and arranged. Size, shape, and the use of space are important format consider-ations. Specific use and the needs of specific users of an information prod-uct are likewise important format considerations. For example, will community bulletin board postings be adequate for the dissemination of map and location information about a service?

The types of information to be presented are also important in format consideration. Will the design of a community information bulletin board attract and hold the attention of a young audience? If not, what improve-ments are needed to garner that attention? The information quality, amount of information, and the design quality of the text are also a part of for-mat. For example, too often bulletin board postings become places for items intended for casual and short-term use, without much consideration of their visual impact. Remember that all designs, including the bulletin board, must be carefully considered for their overall visual impact. This includes the amount of information, placement and spacing of information, major captions of information, type fonts and labeling of information, and its use.[8]

Design Elements

Elements of design include, among others, line, fonts, color, shape, bal-ance, and placement of items. Lines are often used to create mood, to help with organization, to add to texture and design interests, to give direction to the information in terms of information set, and to provide learning cues.[9] Type fonts also are used to set mood and to add interest to the information product. Type fonts help with acquiring and remembering information be-cause they can set information boundaries and act as important learning cues through the select use of size and style and the application of techniques, such as boldface, italics, and colors.[10] Shape helps convey design concepts and can be used to indicate information. For example, highway signs often use color and shape to indicate certain types of information. Black and white rectangular road signs in the United States commonly give road informa-tion; red signs convey warnings; and brown, blue, or green signs offer in-formation about public service areas, such as libraries and museums. Other commonly recognized symbols include signs for danger, radiation, caution, and direction. (See Figure 5.4.)

Like other elements discussed previously, balance can create mood and design impact and interest. This is accomplished through the appropriate use of symmetrical and asymmetrical placements. For example, asymmetrical placement can create tension in the design, thus promoting interest.

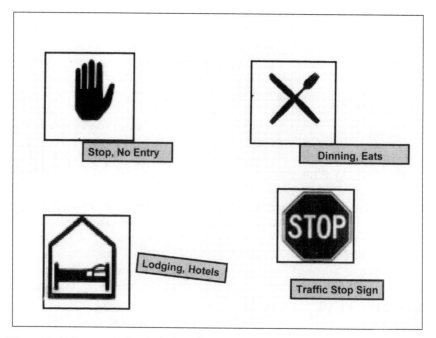

Figure 5.4 Shape and Symbols in Information Product Design

Audience attention can be achieved through design contrast. Contrast can also strengthen ideas and information points and can act as a means of encouraging information retention though the use of learning cues, such as shapes, color, type fonts, and textures. (See Figure 5.5.)

Information design needs a strong sense of unity, which greatly enhances the remembering of information. Information set and boundaries (often conceptualized as a grid) in design are excellent examples of how unity can promote the acquiring and remembering of information. With the use of learning cues and prompts of various kinds, unity of design can lead the user through the information elements in a way that best processes the information. That is, the end of the product is tightly concluded with no ambiguity left.[11] Figure 5.6 illustrates these concepts.

The role of value and color are important in information product design as they are closely allied with how information boundaries and sets are accomplished and how learning cues and prompts are employed. Value is the lightness or darkness of an item. Value can create movement, direction, and intensity; it can set mood and tone. Color adds dimension to value. As we have seen, color and value are important learning cues and prompts. Color

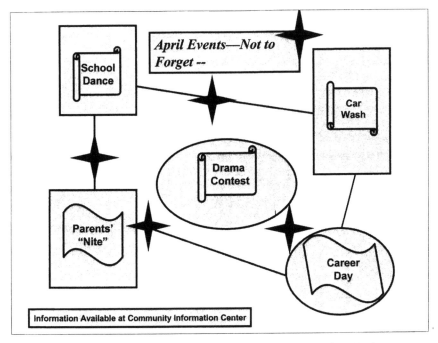

Figure 5.5 Balance, Mood, and Contrasts in Information Product Design

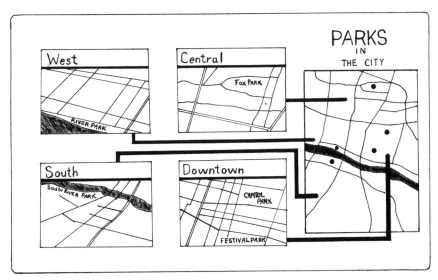

Figure 5.6 Line, Placement, and Balance in Information Product Design. Graphic design concept by Regina Serrambana. Courtesy of In the Galleries, Austin, Texas.

Figure 5.7 Color Values Design

adds emotion, sets mood, and draws attention to important information elements.[12] In information design, like all other elements of design, color and value are always carefully selected to complement and enhance the overall effectiveness of informational products. (See Figures 5.7 and 5.8.)

Figure 5.8 Color Values and Emotional Impact. Courtesy of Out Youth Austin.

Structure, Design, and Application

Structure puts all the design elements together to form a unified and appealing information product design. In terms of their application to community information, all these principles have immediate use in designing community information bulletin boards, developing websites, and designing more appealing, effective forms of information products. Vertical files, picture or graphic collections, and archives can all benefit from these principles.

PART 2. STRATEGIES FOR COMMUNITY INFORMATION DELIVERY

There are several ways that community information can be delivered. This section will discuss some of the most common: the community information bulletin board, the vertical or information file, picture/graphic files, the community information directory, the website, archives, and the referral aspects of community information.

The Community Information Bulletin Board

According to Robert Heinich and his colleagues, bulletin boards were originally designed to feature brief news announcements, urgent notices, and items of immediate interest. Today, in addition to these purposes, they offer decoration or atmospheric purposes, public recognition purposes, and the meeting of educational and training objectives.[13] Brake, in his study of community information in British schools, noted that a community bulletin board can be used to promote materials of interest to students, such as entertainment, music, sports, clubs and societies, careers news, and advice and counseling resources.[14]

The Detroit Public Library's TIP service uses a community bulletin board in a similar fashion to alert and inform the staff of current happenings. For example, local news sources, such as newspapers, can be scanned daily and important notices placed on the board in a systematic fashion with the staff being advised to take notice of new postings. Items placed on the bulletin board often have lasting value. Realizing this, the TIP staff places a note on items that will be moved to the vertical file or information file when their current information usefulness has passed.

Brake also noted that the community bulletin board needs to be aesthetically pleasing.[15] In meeting its goals of being both aesthetically pleasing and a vehicle of information dissemination, a bulletin board's construction and maintenance must reflect principles of information and graphic design, as noted previously in this chapter. Most authorities emphasize the importance of the following aspects of design: space, shape, texture, size, line, arrangement, color, background, borders, and lettering.[16] In addition, learning cues and prompts and an understanding of psychological perceptions as outlined previously can enhance the effectiveness of a community information bulletin board.

THE VERTICAL/INFORMATION FILE

The construction and purpose of the vertical file was discussed in chapter 2. This section will consider some of the organizational features that can be used to make the vertical file a useful community information tool.

SUBJECT AND NAME AUTHORITY CONTROL

As with any file, attention must be paid to consistency in selection and application of terms and proper names. To ensure consistency, both a name and subject authority file must be maintained. This is often accomplished at the local level by adding notes to a commercially published list of subject headings, such as *Sears List of Subject Headings.* An authority file can be an in-house file that grows and develops as the file grows. Generally speaking, published lists of subject headings intended for book collections are not adequate for the specific nature of local community information. With care, an in-house subject and name authority file should not be too difficult to maintain. The following are examples of how subject authority entries can be established and controlled in an in-house subject authority file.

Examples and Applications

- Local School Topics Subject Authority Control:
  Example 1.
    Johnson City High School. Athletics. (A–Z).
    [Here are entered subjects that relate to athletics at Johnson City High School. Topics may be entered A-Z as needed.]
    —Baseball
    —Boxing
    —Football
    —Golf
    Related term(s): **Health Program, Physical Education Program**
  Example 2.
    Johnson City High School. Academic Departments and Programs. (A–Z).
    [Note. Here are entered subjects that relate to academic departments and programs at Johnson City High School. Topics may be entered A–Z as needed.]
    —Art
    —English and Language Arts
    —Social Sciences
    (Scope note: This department includes History, Government, Psychology, and Sociology.)
    Related term(s): **Johnson City High School. Athletics.** (A–Z).

- Local Area Subject Authority Control
  Example 1.
    Smith County, Texas. Youth Organizations and Programs. (A–Z).
    [Note: Here are entered items that relate to youth organizations and programs
    located in Smith County, Texas. Topics may be added A–Z as needed.]
    —Smith County Club for Boys and Girls
    —4-H Clubs (Smith County, Texas). (A–Z).
    —Tyler Public Library Youth Programs. (A–Z).
- Proper Name Authority Control:
  Example 1.
    Doe, John Henry, 1910-1980. Principal of Johnson High School, 1940 to
    1960.
    [Note: Refer from **Doe, John, 1910-1980.** Principle of Johnson High School.
    File in **Johnson City High School. Biography** (A–Z).]

Another approach is to further subdivide the biography section into categories, as indicated below:

Example 2.
  Doe, John Henry , 1910-1980. Principal of Johnson High School, 1940
  to 1960. Refer from **Doe, John, 1910-1980**, Principal of Johnson High
  School. [Note: File in **Johnson City High School. Biography. Principals.**
  (A–Z).]

Often libraries publish their vertical file list on the Internet, and this always provides examples that can be adapted for the local vertical file. For
example, the list used by Louisiana State University for its microfilmed vertical file holdings is available at www.lib.lsu.edu/special/guides/vertical.html.
Special vertical file lists are also available. For example, the vertical file list
of the Science and Technology Library at the University of Manitoba is available on the Internet at http://www.umanitoba.ca/libraries/units/science/
vertical.html.

PICTURE/GRAPHICS FILES

As discussed in chapter 2, the picture file or graphic file has always played
an important role in the school library media center collections and resources.
It has many advantages for the school library media specialist in building
suitable resources. Graphic materials are generally inexpensive and readily
obtainable and are available in many formats ranging from microscope slides
to reproductions of fine art. Educational graphics have traditionally focused
on still pictures, drawings, charts, graphs, posters, and art prints. Graphic
materials can also include exhibits, displays, dioramas, and computer images.
Graphic images of community information, such as historic homes and places,
local geographic features, and individuals, have always been important in
graphic files. Graphic items are easy to use in terms of instruction, and with

supportive technologies, they are easily reproduced. From an instructional point of view, they greatly add perceptions about reality and can correct mistaken concepts.[17] For most of these items, cataloging rules and processing procedures have been developed and widely disseminated. MARC format records are generally available for most graphic formats and computer cataloging systems that focus on the school library media center online catalogs needs. The well-known program "MARC, Magician" can accommodate most graphic formats.[18]

Graphic images in digitized formats are now common and can play a significant role alongside the more traditional printed forms of graphic materials. Digitized graphics, including community resources, are available from computer systems and from the Internet, and they can be produced locally with scanners and digital cameras.

Educator Jamie McKenzie advocates that school media center specialties develop an electronic archive of photographs to support the curriculum. McKenzie believes that such an archive can be stored on the school server and displayed through the school's website. Like the more traditional "picture file," this file too must be organized by appropriate subject headings.[19] McKenzie maintains that this will require that "meta tags" or keywords that are appropriate for the database be developed and attached to the images in the file so that precise retrieval of graphics can be achieved. Art museums and historical societies often maintain excellent picture or graphic collections and can serve as guides to organizational structure as well as offer suggestions for subject headings. Some examples include the following:

The Fine Arts Museums of San Francisco
    http://www.thinker.org/fam/index_ thinker.asp
The Pennsylvania Colony of Nebraska Historical Society
    http://penncolony nebraska.org/pictures/pics_panoramas3_02.htm
Conway Historical Society, Conway, New Hampshire
    http://www.conwayhistory. org/conway_photos1.html
Portage County (Wisconsin) Historical Society Photo Collection
    http://library. uwsp.edu/pchs/
Austin (Texas) History Center
    http://www.ci.austin.tx.us/library/ahc/green/default.htm

McKenzie suggests that a "turn-key" graphic cataloging system is useful for organizing graphics.[20] For example, "Extensis" is a recommended system that catalogs images and also allows publishing of images to a website (http://www.extensis.com/portfolio/31g.html).[21] Less expensive systems are produced by Ulread (http://www.ulead.com) and Nova Development (www.novadevelopment.com). Tucows Inc., an Internet wholesale service company (www.tucows.com), also offers affordable photo editing programs for purchase and review. These include BR's PhotoArchiver, Easy Thumbnails, and Archive Creator. To increase the viability of a graphic collection, a scanner and a video camera are necessary. In addition, if the center has collections of older videocassettes of local events, a photo-editing program capable of extracting selected images from videotapes is also recommended.

THE LIBRARY WEBSITE AND COMMUNITY INFORMATION

School library media center websites are now common and are fast becoming an expected element in the resources provided by programs. For the most part, these sites tend to reflect the immediate interest of the school community and focus largely on what goes on within the school. Typically, these sites reinforce the school mission and curriculum, and include resources that support the curriculum and information about the school district. Sometimes, school library media center websites will link to outside sources, such as the local public library and government agencies, that offer curriculum support. Examples of such websites are provided below.

At this writing, few school websites link to what is generally considered community information. If the public library in the area offers community information and the center links to such a site, then community information is available, but it is not common to find websites that link directly to community information. The Spring Branch Independent School District near Houston offers an extensive website, but it does not link directly to community information. Librarians responsible for this site have indicated that they realize the need for such information and have it under consideration (http://it.springbranchisd.com/library-resources/).[22]

Planning for a school library media center website that links to community information requires consideration of several factors:

- What is the purpose of links to community information, and how can such links be justified within the center's missions, goals, and objectives?
- Who will likely be using these links (parents, teachers, students, staff)?
- What is the identified audience likely to want in terms of community information?
- How will community links be reviewed and selected, and how can they be justified in terms of the center's collection development and materials selection policies?
- Can challenges to links be resolved under existing collection development and materials selection policies?

Construction of Sites

Most school library media websites reside on the servers of the school or district and, in many cases, school library media specialists are the school's webmasters. If not in charge of the school's website, they often manage the school library media center's section of the school's website. In this capacity, the library media specialist can determine the community information links that seem appropriate for the school community.

Authoring tools are the best and most efficient ways to build a website. Widely used commercial authoring tools include FrontPage (http://www.microsoft.com/frontpage/), Dreamweaver, and HomeSite (http://www.macromedia.com/software/homesite/). Dreamweaver, a Macromedia product (http://www.macromedia.com/software/dreamweaver/), offers graphical interface, text and design modes, and tools that facilitate collaboration among designers. Important project management features in the package include link checking. It operates on both Windows and Apple platforms.[23]

Design of the Site

Designing the website requires attention to both text and graphic features. A good design will feature essential information about the site and its suggested resources and links, and it will be easy to navigate. Psychologist and information design authority Andrew Dillon offers some practical advice on electronic text design elements in his book *Designing Usable Electronic Text*.[24]

The first step should be to draft on paper a conceptual view of the site. The site should first offer:

- Clear identification: name, location, address, and contact information (e.g., e-mail address);
- Statement of mission and goals of the school library media center;
- Overview of services offered;
- Identification of person(s) in charge of the site and staff contact information. Personal security does not require the naming of the individual but does necessitate giving the name of an administrative position in charge of the site. For example, a statement such as "Please contact the librarian and webmaster with comments and suggestions" is sufficient.

Graphic design factors are similar to design factors associated with creating any type of information product, as discussed previously in this chapter. Design considerations that relate especially to websites include the following:[25]

- *Colors and Background Textures.* Color selection must be consistently used throughout the website. A consistent color scheme adds to the cohesive look of the site. Color is often associated with information and can be used to reinforce the ease of navigation within the site (e.g., all links in the same color). Use colors that offer contrasts between text and background. For example, avoid a dark blue background with black text. Use no more than three carefully selected colors throughout the site—one background color and two accent colors, applied consistently throughout the site. Avoid patterned or tiled backgrounds. These often conflict with text and make reading difficult. Guides to colors can be found at PageTutor's Color Picker at (http://www.pagetutor.com/pagetutor/ makapage/picker/index.html) and Webmaster's Color Lab at (www.visibone.com/ colorlab/).

- *Fonts, Texts, and Placement.* Select and use only one or two fonts throughout the site. Use one font type for headers and another for text. Break the text into meaningful sections or small units with headings. Avoid running text completely across the screen. Make sure that the information is carefully spaced and avoid information clutter. Do not use multicolor text as that generally creates confusion. (See Figure 5.9.)
- *Images.* For quick downloading, use small and compressed (thumbnail) images and specify the image size and format (e.g., .gif, .jpg, .png). Remember that some users will not accept images, so make sure that text alternatives are available.
- *Accessibility for Those with Disabilities.* Consideration of the special needs of those with disabilities is necessary. Special website design tools are available to help people with special needs to access websites. Audio or video segments should provide access to text captions. Images should use an alt tag to provide text. Some type of information, such as graphs or charts, should be summarized, and blinking and flashing content should be avoided. Consult IBM for suggestions on how to meet accessibility needs (http://www-3.ibm.com/able/).
- *Review and Test-Market Your Site.* Before you mount your site, make sure that it is reviewed by potential users. Be ready to revise the site based on well-informed

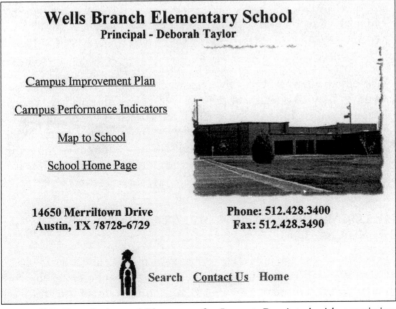

Figure 5.9 Font Styles and Placement for Impact. Reprinted with permission from www.roundrockisd.org.

suggestions. A free software tool that permits you to check your pages and monitor them for accessibility is available at www.cast.org/bobby/.

Linkage to Community Information

Community information links on the center's website will need to be well marked. It is appropriate to designate a space in the site for community information. For example, a link can be stated in the following ways:

"Browse the community . . ."
Here, links to community web resources should be attached. Most communities already have sites available that can be conveniently linked, such as general community pages and links to county and city government sites.

"Browse information centers and links in our community . . ."
Provide here a subject list of information centers available in the community such as Children's Centers, Jobs and Career Centers, and Community Information Networks. Specific links can be embedded within these broad subject headings. Another approach is to list each community resource separately or within a large related groups of links. The advantage here is that each site can be reviewed separately and added according to existing selection policies in terms of how it suits the needs of the center.

"Explore our community . . ."
This approach allows for community information to be displayed by themes and relates events occurring in the community. For example, certain organizations may have developed a special theme site around events that occur in the community. This might include a local celebration, a food walk campaign, or celebration of a national holiday. Such sites can be linked on the page as long as they remain timely.

Visit public library websites that link to community information for suggestions on how to design and present community information. These are easily found on the Internet using search terms such as "public library community information." The Public Library Association of the American Library Association maintains a discussion group called Community Information Services that has ongoing publication and education programs regarding community information (http://www.spiretech.com/~dreed/pla-cis/).

THE LOCAL INFORMATION DIRECTORY AND THE ONLINE CATALOG

Experience from the public library has shown that a directory of community resources and information is useful and probably necessary for a well-run community information system. Brake, in his study of how to develop a community information service in British schools, suggested that an index to community resources was one of several components necessary for a complete community information delivery system. Public libraries have traditionally provided such directories in several ways. Before the age of computers, a three-by-five-inch card file was often used. This worked in the past and continues to work well if the directory is small and is likely to remain small. Libraries have also used printed directories, which are expensive but can represent an array of community resources. Production expenses and the fact that a printed directory is hard to update and keep current are two of its primary disadvantages. The widespread use of computers has made it possible for community information directory information to be placed in the online catalog. As noted, school library cataloging systems rarely accommodate such formats, but the USMARC formats do provide for a variety of community information records, and many libraries now maintain their community information records online using the MARC formats.

Some public libraries have assumed the responsibility of developing and maintaining a directory of community organizations. They do this by first developing a form that can accommodate information about organizations and then invite organizations to fill out the form so that the information can be added to their online database. The invitation to join the directory is often placed on the library's community information website. An example of such an invitation and form is available at the Baltimore County Public Library (http://carlweb.bcpl.lib.md.us/cgi-bin/cw_cgi?getBasicTerms+17693).

THE ARCHIVES

School archives and community information seem to be a natural connection. Archives are "the noncurrent records of an organization or institution preserved because of their continued value," and archives include all physical items that in some way have been used to convey information. This includes media such as paper, film, photographs, audio and video, computer files, and digitized images.[26] The general organizational pattern suggested for archives is *provenance* or source of origin. That is to say, archival materials are kept together under the body that created them (office, agency, institution, person). Items are not intermixed regardless of how they might relate subject-wise to items created by another body.[27] At the local school-building level, an archive might be limited to only selected types of records and will not attempt to collect the entire archives of the school. A comprehensive records management and archival program is more the responsibility of the school system and should be handled at the district level.

Archives often specialize in what they collect and preserve. One archive might decide to emphasize local history and biography while another might focus its effort on collecting regional or cultural geography. Institutional archives generally collect and preserve the records of the parent body. With this latitude in mind, at the local school-building level, an archival program might concentrate on certain themes or activities. For example, art, music, sports, and literary activities of students and teachers might lend themselves well to a local school archives.

With the help of others in the school community, the school library media specialists can:

- Develop a plan for the archive. This plan should include what is to be collected. A practical step would be to develop an inventory of activities that take place in the school and seem worthy of preserving and are of historical importance. Place those in priority, considering interests and their historical importance. From that list and with the advice of others, decide what should be collected.
- Decide who will administer the program and how. In the context of this discussion, the school library media specialist seems to be the logical administrator.
- Decide where it will be located, making sure that adequate physical space is available.
- Make sure that ongoing support is available. This includes both financial and administrative commitment.
- Develop a plan for collection development. How will materials be located and acquired in a systematic way? Appraisal is an important factor in collection development. Not all groups of records produced by an agency or activity need to be added to an archive. Appraisal is a process whereby groups of records are analyzed for "enduring historical, legal, administrative, or fiscal value . . . [in relation] to their relationships with other groups of records. Not all records merit permanent retention in the archives."[28]
- Organize the archival collection based on standard archival principles. Arrangement in an archive is based on provenance and, if possible, original order is maintained. This is how the materials are arranged both intellectually and physically for access. Without going into excessive details, a building-level archive can be organized according to "Record Groups," and materials related to that group would then be divided into appropriate series and file units. For example:

Record Group 1. Springdale High School.
Science Department
   District Science Projects Competitions. 1960.
   Rules and Regulations
   [Includes official rules and regulations for the 1960 competition.]
Student Projects (A–Z)
   [Note: Includes examples of students project submitted for competition. Items include photoprints of exhibits and printed explanations of science projects.]
Speech and Drama Department
   Public Play Performances, 1960–1961.
   Programs and Announcements.
   [Note: Includes printed official programs of plays performed for the general public, 1960–1961. Also includes official advertisement copy and announcements.]

- Once the collection has been organized, it should be described. Description is written information about the collection or record group. Generally, a description will begin with a history of the collection or record group with notes and suggestions about its contents and usefulness for certain types of research and information needs. Finding aids can include guides and brochures to the entire archives; inventory accession records, detailing when and how records were obtained; analysis, history, and function of the office or program; descriptive notes of the contents; listings of folders within the group; and an item calendar.[29]

- Policies and procedures concerning reference and access to items, supervision and control of materials, outreach programs and marketing of the archives, and preservation and physical protection of materials are other important elements to be considered.[30]

The school-building level archival program can be as extensive or as limited as necessary based on an assessment of needs and support available for the program. An archival program at the district level needs to be more extensive in order that the records of the school be available for researchers in a systematically organized pattern. Whether at the local or district level, archives reflect community information and resources, and should not be overlooked in planning a community information program.

Many useful and practical guides are available for help in organizing and maintaining a local history and community archive. For example, the "How-to-Do" series published by Neal-Schuman (www.neal-schuman.com) offers *Developing and Maintaining Practical Archives* by Gregory S. Hunter (2003); and *Building Digital Archives, Description & Display* by Frederick Stielow (2003).

The Austin Public Library's Austin History Center website offers a listing of its many services. This listing reflects the array of services that a local archive can offer its public. For an overview of such services, visit its site at http://www.ci.austin.tx.us/library/ahc/collect.htm.

The Center has developed several guides for helping individuals care for their personal archives and media. These guides are not only beneficial to individuals but can also help school library media specialists. These include "Caring for Books and Other Paper Based Materials," "Caring for Audiotapes," "Caring for Videotapes," "Caring for Your Family Photographs," and "Starting an Archive." These are free upon request from the Center. Requests for copies should be addressed to Austin History Center, Austin Public Library, 810 Guadalupe Street, Austin, Texas 78701.

The Center has also published its collection development policy and its processing manual online. For these, visit http://www.ci.austin.tx.us/library/ahc/downloads/ahc_collection_development_policy.doc and http://www.wiredforyouth.com/downloads/archivesmanual4_6.doc.

In addition, the Center provides useful links to other resources helpful to school library media specialists on the care and preservation of materials, such as "Creating Scrapbooks" by Ralph McKnight (http://www.ci.austin.tx.us/library/ahc/psv.htm).

PROTECTING AND CONSERVING MATERIALS

Some materials obtained for the community information program may not be of lasting value and do not need to be saved and preserved. Nevertheless, often what seem to be routine items may indeed be important for social, cultural, organizational, or historical reasons, thus requiring that attention be given to their storage and preservation. As discussed in chapter 3, retention of such materials is based on assessment consideration and objectives stated in a school's overall materials selection and collection development policies. For example, a newspaper clipping calling attention to a concert of a significant performer and first placed on the community information bulletin board may have lasting value and might be useful in the vertical or information file after it has served its immediate use as an item of notification. Once the decision has been made to retain the materials for the long term, materials must be stored and preserved.

Most, if not all, of the materials acquired for the community information program are in print or electronic form, and they each have requirements for storage and preservation. The Austin History Center of the Austin Public Library recommends that materials of lasting value be carefully preserved. The following is a list of their suggestions:

- Store materials in a stable environment, below 75 degrees Fahrenheit and 50 percent humidity. Avoid unnecessary light.
- All materials should be protected by encasing them in acid-free boxes, folders, and sleeves, including non-stick plastic covers for photographic items.
- When mounting individual items, use acid-free paper and archival mounts.
- Newspapers clippings must also be copied onto acid-free paper.
- PVC-free polypropylene page protectors should be used for separating and protecting individual pages.
- Acid-free buffer tissue paper should be used to isolate acidic items, such as newsprint, from other items.
- For adhesives, use glue sticks, starch paste, or methyl cellule. Never use tape of any kind (masking, transparent, or removable) or rubber cement.
- Use acid-free labels for folders and other containers.
- Each item must be identified and dated. Append this directly to the item itself. In order not to deface the item, place this identification in a safe place not likely to interfere with the image or other types of information (e.g., at the top, bottom, or back of the item).
- Identify with dates all images and information items (if not readily available from content) including places, building, events, locations, and people.
- When applying identification, use soft pencils and use only acid-free matting materials. Use a window mat to hold photos and drawings away from glass.
- For fragile or brittle photographs and similar types of items, brace these with acid-free supporters.
- Store items unfolded or unrolled.
- Remove staples (if staples are used, make sure they are stainless-steel staples), paper clips, and rubber bands.

- Do not use ballpoint pens for any type of marking.
- Do not write on paper that rests on items (e.g., books, photos, documents).
- Avoid touching the image sides of photos or the dull side of negatives.
  (http://www.ci.austin.tx.us/library/ahc/preserve.htm)

Electronic digitization can preserve some of these materials. Guidance and standards on how this can be accomplished are offered by The Library of Congress as well as other organizations. The Council on Library and Information Resources presents a guide to digital preservation.[31] Websites that provide preservation information include Conservation OnLine (http://palimpsest.stanford.edu) and The Library of Congress Preservation Page (http://www.ci.austin.tx.us/library/ahc/preserve.htm).

REFERRALS AND GIVING ADVICE

Community information often requires that referrals be made to other agencies. This tradition arose within social work where requests for information necessitated helping the client to receive help from agencies and even advocate for the client for services and help. Libraries have generally elected to gather and record resources and to direct clients to appropriate agencies where more involved information and help can be obtained:

> The Public Library I&R [e.g., Information and Referral/Community Information] provides information—not advice. The referral role means assisting the patron to get to the source or sources that are qualified to give advice.[32]

Referral and advice giving within a school library media center must always conform to the policies and procedures of the school district and school.

CONCLUSION

Community information is diverse and the ways and means of providing this information are diverse as well. A library can elect to have a simple system or an elaborate one, depending on local needs, resources, and support. This chapter has considered some of the many avenues available for consideration. Because community information has had a long history within the public library, its adoption by school media centers is not difficult. Based on a survey of the literature and observations, the concept of community information in a school library media center is relatively new and untried. As it should, curriculum drives the school library media program. Curriculum in the modern school is expanding and becoming much more inclusive of the world and the local community. Technology and expanding world and cultural concepts will likely ensure that community information become more vital to students' lives and to their learning.

NOTES

1. Karen DeBord and Millie Ferrer, "Working with Latino Parents/Families." Available at www.cyfernet.org/parent/latinofam.html. Accessed March 19, 2003.

2. Malcolm Fleming and Howard Levie, *Instructional Message Design* (Englewood Cliffs, N.J.: Educational Technology Publications, 1978), 3–18.

3. Ibid., 17–18.

4. Ibid., 12–14, 18, 54, 188.

5. Ibid., 101.

6. Ibid., 28.

7. Ibid., 11–12.

8. Bryan Peterson, *Using Design Basics to Get Creative Results* (Cincinnati: North Light Books, 1996), 17–23.

9. Ibid., 26–30.

10. Ibid., 31–37.

11. Ibid., 50–68.

12. Ibid., 69–77.

13. Robert Heinich and others, *Instructional Media and Technologies for Learning*, 6th ed. (Upper Saddle River, N.J.: Merrill, 1999), 117–18.

14. Terence Brake, *The Need to Know: Teaching the Importance of Information*. Final Report for the Period January 1978–March 1979. (London: The British Library, 1980), 17.

15. Ibid., 17.

16. Karen Hawthorne and Jane E. Gibson, *Bulletin Boards and 3-D Showcases That Capture Them with Pizzazz* (Englewood, Colo.: Libraries Unlimited, 1999), 3–10.

17. Robert Heinich and others, 108–26; Phyllis J. Van Orden and Kay Bishop, *The Collection Program in Schools: Concepts, Practices, and Information Sources,* 3rd ed. (Englewood, Colo.: Libraries Unlimited, 2001), 160–62.

18. Arlene G. Taylor, *Wynar's Introduction to Cataloging and Classification*, 9th ed. (Englewood, Colo.: Libraries Unlimited, 2000), 147–60.

19 . Jamie McKenzie, "The New Vertical File: Delivering Great Images and Data to the Desktop," *FNO: From Now On, The Educational Technology Journal* 10 (October 2000), accessed March 4, 2003, available at http://www.fno.org/oct00/vertical.html.

20. Ibid.

21 . Ibid.

22. W. B. Lukenbill, Question to Spring Branch Librarian Panel, Texas Library Association Conference, April 2003.

23. Anne Martinez, *Cheap Web Tricks!: Build and Promote a Successful Web Site Without Spending a Dime* (New York: Osborne/McGraw-Hill, 2001), 73.

24. Andrew Dillon, *Designing Usable Electronic Text,* 2nd ed. (Boca Raton, Fla.: CRC Press, 2003).

25. Martinez, 84–102.

26. Elizabeth Yakel, *Starting an Archives* (Metuchen, N.J.: Society of American Archivists and Scarecrow Press, 1994), 1.

27. Ibid., 39.

28. Ibid., 15.

29. Ibid., 41–44.

30. Ibid., 47–68.

31. *Building and Sustaining Digital Collections: Models for Libraries and Museums* (Washington, D.C.: Council on Library and Information Resources, 2001).

32. Clara. J. Jones, ed., *Public Library Information and Referral Service* (Syracuse, N.Y.: Gaylord, 1978), 29.

CHAPTER 6

Models and Issues

INTRODUCTION

This chapter discusses some existing models and procedures for establishing a viable community information service in the school library media center. It also considers some important issues and problems that must be faced in the management of school-based community information systems in the school library media center. These include critical thinking skills as applied to community information; accessibility, censorship, and government control of information; readability and design considerations as selection criteria; and the selection and dissemination of sensitive materials, such as sexuality and mental health information. This chapter will also address how to accommodate the role of advocacy and counseling associated with community information within a school library media center environment and how to protect the individual's right to privacy in terms of his or her information needs and requests.

MODELS AND PROCEDURES: A BRIEF HISTORY

Community information programs are not entirely new. As early as the 1860s and 1870s in the United States, charity organizations were helping people find assistance using referrals and other forms of assistance. This was especially noticeable in settlement houses and in neighborhoods affected by poverty. In 1912, the United Way in Cleveland established a community directory service and in 1914 the American Red Cross also established a community information-type training program. The years just preceding and following World War II in Britain produced a great deal of interest and activities involving community information. Citizens' Advice Bureaus were created in the British Isles (England, Scotland, and North Wales) to help families affected by the dislocation of war. In 1946 in the United States, the U.S. Veterans' Information Centers were formed to help returning veterans find suitable housing and work.[1]

Social changes taking place in the 1960s afforded public libraries the opportunity to consider more deeply the information needs of people. Among the first programs to seriously address the need for community information was the federally funded Public Information Center operated by the Enoch Pratt Public Library in cooperation with the School of Library and Information Service of the University of Maryland.[2] The Urban Neighborhood Information Center Project was another. From 1972 to 1975, five major public libraries (Atlanta, Cleveland, Detroit, Houston, and Queens Borough, New York) participated in this partially federally funded experimental program. Each of these libraries conducted different community information programs, some of which were more successful and long-lasting than others. Overall, they demonstrated that public libraries could play an effective role in community information.[3] In a 1975 study, Thomas Childers evaluated the success of these programs. Among his findings were that administrative support and informing other staff members about the role that community information and I&R played within the total library's program were essential for success.[4] In 1984, Thomas Childers continued his research, again funded by the U.S. Office of Education, into community information and I&R services being offered by American public libraries at the time of his investigation.[5] In this study he analyzed programs in Memphis, Colorado Springs, Dallas, Amherst, Baltimore County, San Mateo County, and Caroline County (Maryland), making comparisons between what he termed the characteristics of "high and low profile" programs.[6]

As indicated from the history previously given, the 1970s were filled with activism designed to test the roles that libraries might play in providing community information. Influenced by the rapid increase in information centers serving ordinary citizens, in the late 1970s, the British Library turned its attention to testing the role of community information in schools and school libraries.[7]

THE BRITISH LIBRARY MODEL

In 1978–1979, the British Library funded a study at the South Hackney School in inner-city London to help answer questions about students' needs for information. The study was based on the assumption that schoolchildren in poor, urban areas needed special assistance to help them cope with modern life.[8] The three major questions asked in the study were:

- What sorts of information do young people need while at school and after they leave school?
- What information sources are able to supply the relevant information?
- What information skills should pupils acquire before leaving school?

With those questions in mind, the researchers assessed the information sources that where available in the school's service area ("catchment area of the school"); they organized the information in vehicles so it could be retrieved and placed those devices in the school library, and they created trial community information teaching units designed to be taught by classroom teachers to fourth-year students for a period of ten weeks.

An assumption made in the study was that children from poor, urban areas were basically isolated in the city, and special intervention was necessary to help them cope with the demands of everyday life. Further rationale for this study was based on the rapid change in community life and the complexity of social life. This included the rapid increase in the number and role of community information centers, the rise of community politics, the change and redevelopment of urban centers directed and influenced by government policy, and the creation of numerous information centers and services that grew from that. The complexity of society suggested to the researchers that older forms of information, such as friends, family, and neighbors, were not enough to meet complex information needs. The researchers' reasons were that such traditional social networking generally offered superficial and unreliable information. The researchers asserted that special information skills were now required to negotiate the complex urban world in which youth find themselves. Government and organizational bureaucracy, shopping and involvement in retail, work organizations, leisure and its commercialization all required sophisticated skills.

To exist successfully in an urban world, the study suggested that students needed to see the close relationship between correct information and decision-making. Assuming that library-user education was inadequate for the task, the study outlined the following relationships:

- Important (Chief) Skills and Skills Required for Good Decision-Making:
  - Identify all available alternations to a decision;
  - Identify the information needed to choose between the various alternatives;
  - Evaluate possible sources of information.
- Information Required for Good Decision-Making:
  - Obtain and consider information about possible alternative actions;
  - Obtain and consider information on possible outcomes;
  - Consider information on the probability of projected outcomes;
  - Consider information on the desirability of outcomes.

The teaching units were developed around these four concepts:

- What do I need to know? [problem formation, need identification, information perspective in terms of how to manage problems]
- Where do I find it? [function and sources of information in the community, neighborhood, and school; development of skills to use available information]
- What does it mean? [perception of relevance, adequacy, critical understanding of information; values in the interpretation of information]
- What do I do now? [illumination of the importance of information in making decisions; encouragement of informed decision-making]

The following information delivery model (see Figure 6.1) was developed to reinforce the instructional plan, excluding the computer, it consisted of a literature file, an information notice board (bulletin board), giveaway materials, directories, and local card information index or directory.

Regarding the teaching program, Brake noted that the materials were well received by both teachers and pupils, but that more work was needed in fine-tuning in terms of materials, time, and presentations. The researcher did note that it was difficult for students to formulate an "informational problem" and to see a relationship between community information and formal school knowledge. Because the program was not a port of the British centralized

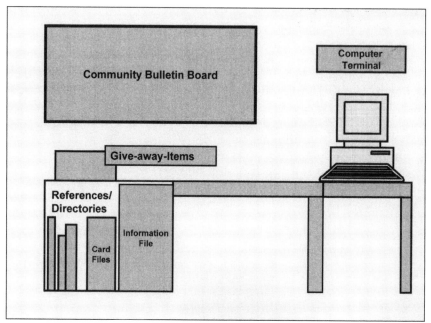

Figure 6.1 The British Library Community Information School Library Model. Published by permission from The British Library.

examination subjects, some students did not take the program seriously. Some teachers felt that they needed better training in how to teach community information and that it needed to be better planned in terms of integration into the curriculum.

The importance of this study is that it is the first field investigation into the use of community information in a school environment, offering insight and suggestions for the better integration of community information in school settings. Its general recommendations are especially helpful. Among these are:[9]

- Rethink traditional library-user education to better integrate these instructions into everyday classroom teaching.
- Community information must translate terms and concepts into the everyday language and experiences of students.
- Community information instruction can be given in schools, but it also has a place in other, less formal youth services agencies, such as clubs and counseling centers.
- Research is needed regarding the effectiveness of information systems that serve youth and how those can be made better within educational systems.
- Research is needed into the information-seeking (and information-avoiding) behaviors of youth. This includes both formal and informal social networks that offer information, the effects of geographic location of information sources, and cultural diversities found in society.
- Social agencies other than schools and libraries must be encouraged to consider community information as a vital part of their service programs. Better cooperation and communication is needed between community agencies, schools, and public libraries.
- Community information programs in school must be based on considerable prior planning and supported by a network of local information workers (e.g., librarians, teachers, social workers, etc.).
- Teaching materials must be effective. Resource bibliographies in the theory and practice of community information are needed. Instructional materials must be well designed with use by intended audiences carefully considered. Commercial publishers should be encouraged to produce community information instructional packages.
- Other agencies in society, such as radio and television broadcasting, should be encouraged to participate by offering community information programs.

Although these suggestions were made over twenty years ago, many of them still await action.

CONCERNS AND OPINIONS FROM THE FIELD: A RESEARCH REPORT

Models and processes used in any profession can be improved by knowing what is needed and accepted by the field at large. Of course, questions exist within such contexts. In order to make an attempt at answering some of these questions and to assess what might be happening in the field, the author and his associate, Belinda Boon, conducted several field investigations. One was an informal inquiry sent to LM_NET, in February 2003, the second was a field assessment using a small focus group of eight school and public librarians drawn from the Austin, Texas, area, and the third was a convenience survey based on a questionnaire distributed to both public and school librarians attending workshops in the summer and fall of 2003.

Responses from an Informal LN_NET Inquiry

In February 2003, the author and his associate, Belinda Boon, sent out an inquiry on LM_NET asking for information regarding how community information might be managed in school library media centers. The following questions were asked:

- Does your library provide community information, and if so, in what formats (e.g., pictures, materials from community organizations, vertical or information file items, indexes to community resources, links to websites in the community, directories of community information)?
- Do you have mechanisms established for acquiring community information (e.g., means to gather information about community resources, ways to assess and review contacts and recommendations, etc.)?
- How do you maintain online community information resources from the Internet (e.g., policies on selection, access, updating and currency, restrictions and removal of restrictions, censorship questions)?

Although only three usable responses were received, they were revealing and are presented below with slight editorial modifications:

Response 1. (Elementary school, location not given)
At my previous school (middle school) [we] kept brochures, articles, etc. about community resources in a vertical file. Nothing like that existed in the elementary school that I came to this year, but the school lobby contains brochures from a fairly large number of community groups relevant to the parents and students. We have no mechanisms established for acquiring community information nor do we maintain links to community information from the Internet.
Response 2. (High school in New York State)
We keep lists of organizations, museums, and public officials; our pictures collections consist largely of books and brochures purchased for the collection. We include news articles on local events and issues in the vertical file; on our website, we provide various links to community information and change these frequently as need demands. Local information is gathered by the school library media specialists who contact or visit local people and places. All website maintenance is handled by me, the school library media specialist.

Response 3. (High school in Iowa)

We do not distribute materials from community organizations nor provide directories of community organizations; we keep local newspapers that focus upon unusual or important events, such as school sport championships. Our library has a number of community booklets that are cataloged and shelved in the reference collection. We do not keep a vertical file in the traditional sense of the term. On our web page we provide links to community resources in the valley. These links are based on recommendations from several sources or are discovered by the library staff as we build our website. We also provide an information link to our alumni. We encourage alumni to email the website with their information, which is then reviewed and posted.

We have guidelines for our website. For example, we do not permit links from for-profit-organizations; we also remove inactive links as we find them. Our web page states that all items posted conform to and follow the school board's selection policy.

Themes Posed to the Focus Group

The focus group was conducted by Belinda Boon, a professional library consultant and trainer. The question presented to the focus group centered on these themes:

- How do you define community?
- Do you accept a standard, professional definition of community information?
- What kinds of community information do you now provide?
- How is community information generally organized in school library media centers?
- How can or might community information be promoted and marketed within a school media library setting?
- What types of community information is or might be needed in a school library media environment?
- What kinds of requests are made or might be made that can be categorized as community information?
- How involved are you now in networking with community groups?
- What are the strengths of offering a community information program within a school library media center?
- What problems can be expected to arise in offering a school library media center-based community information program?
- What staff skills are needed to successfully manage a community information program in a school library media center?
- What experiences, if any, do you personally have with providing community information services?
- In what areas of instruction can information literary be associated with or improved on through community information programs?
- Can you provide any local examples of a community information program operating with school library media programs?

- What recommendations or insights might you offer concerning community information programs in school library media centers?

(See Appendix 3 for questions presented to the focus group with a transcription of responses.)

Reponses from the Focus Group

Defining the Community

The first question asked of the focus group was to give their views of community in terms of whether they saw community as a geographic unit or as a state of mind or image. Several determinants or definitions about community were generated by this question. For example, the modern school community is often represented by students from many cultural origins, bringing with them different languages and cultural experiences. Extended families must also be considered elements in the modern school community, as well as a geographic neighborhood served by the school and the larger school community of teachers, staff, and parents.

The group felt that the school's location within a given geographic boundary also affects how a school community can be defined. A community has both broad and narrow definitions. It is broad in the sense that it must reach beyond the geographic limitations of the school to both connect with and explain social services, such as policies and services available, and it must market and support other cultural support services that exist in the broader community. Community goes beyond geographic boundaries in that the school community must continually work to broaden patrons' mind-sets regarding the idea of community, especially as this mind-set often is limited in its understanding of the social and informational role that libraries play in community life.

Population does tend to influence how people see their community or how they are forced to see their community. People tend to define their community as they define themselves. For example, most of us use age, culture, group, and school populations to define who we are and whom we serve. Size of the community does influence the idea of community, but these other factors probably play a more important role.

As a population grows, by necessity it must become more specialized. This is true for a city or county and for a school system. For example, in a large and complex society, a school might stage a community information fair for parents and other caregivers of students. Within this context, appropriate referrals can be made to a school counselor for social service needs as well as to other school support staff members, such as the school nurse and counselor. At the district level, a school's community resources department can handle more complicated requests and needs coming from both parents and the community at large. For example, in its attempt to help parents understand both the school system and the community at large, the Austin Independent School District (Austin, Texas) offers a Community/School Project whereby people from the community are invited to visit schools, eat lunch in the cafeterias, use the libraries, and gain a sense of ownership of the schools in their communities. In some communities, because of limited resources, the school library becomes the public library.

The Meaning of Community Information

The focus group was asked to consider if they agreed with the following commonly accepted definition of community information:

> A service for providing the community served and individual library users . . . with all pertinent information about and referral to sources that can provide answers to meet their needs for service and assistance. The sources may be government, community, neighborhood or voluntary organizations and institutions, or they may be obtained through the individual.[10]

The group tended to accept this definition, but school librarians in the focus group saw community information as fundamentally connected to curriculum.

Kinds of Community Information Currently Provided in the Library

The focus group was also asked to consider, except for the local newspapers, what types of community information they provided in the school library. Again, the response was that most of the information was curriculum related.

Organization of Community Information

The group was encouraged to rationalize how community information is, could be, or might be organized in their libraries or in libraries that they knew about. The consensus expressed by the group was that the vertical file is going out of style and is not used much any more. Bulletin boards for the public library newsletter announcements and e-mail service able to refer patrons to external services are becoming more popular.

Promotion and Distribution of Community Information

The question of promotion of community information was asked of the groups and succeeded in raising issues associated with the role of the library—whether school or public—in promoting community information sites. The concern arose whether a listing of a community information resource, either on a website or in a newsletter, signified that the library endorsed the site.

For a school library, this can be problematic because often parents feel that if services are highlighted by the library through various distribution means, such as pamphlet giveaways, then the library is endorsing such services. Other ways promote community information, but the best way to guard against such assumptions is to mention and describe services through parents's newsletters, where limitations and special audience needs are addressed. The same is true of forwarding to parents and other parties e-mail announcements received from community groups by the library. The group advised that many of these questions can and should be addressed in the materials selection policy, where examples of appropriate sites are mentioned together with justification for the inclusion of such sites in a community information program.

What Type of Information Is Needed in Your Library?

This question elicited several suggestions, including parenting information, programming information about events at the public library (including bilingual programs), Medicaid information for parents, blood drive information, insurance programs for uninsured children, information about lost animals, items for sale, and sources for public services, such as services provided by police departments and social agencies

Requests for Information

In responding to the questions about the nature of requests made concerning what might be categorized as community information, school librarians in the focus group indicated that parents make the most requests for community information. Occasionally, persons from the community will seek information and will offer to volunteer their services. Most focus group members allowed parents to check out books from their collections.

Networking and Community Groups

The focus group reported that the networking they encounter is largely that of outreach services that they offer the community. For example, for schools, this includes making available a special card that allows senior citizens to use school gyms and to buy food at the cafeteria at a discount. Other school-based outreach programs involve the use of computers, certain library services, and access to English as a Second Language (ESL) courses. Networking also provides information on how and where to take GED examinations.

Strengths of Having Community Information in the School Library Media Center

To this group, curriculum, teaching support, and parental involvement in the school, especially through sharing skills and volunteer services, appeared to be the most important justifications for having community information in the school. School policy dictates the extent to which a school can link to community services in support of curriculum needs.

Problems in Providing Community Information in the School Library Media Center

Several problems were noted by the focus groups for offering community information services. These included cost, insurance, liability, staffing, and security. Costs related to planning and maintenance, the selection of appropriate materials for the collection, and the time required to search for age- and grade-appropriate materials must be considered. Technical needs and their costs, such as server space on computers and web page maintenance time, also are factors that cannot be overlooked. The argument as to whether electronic format or paper source is more effective is also problematic.

Staff Skills

The technical know-how of the staff must be carefully considered. One member of the group noted that to help in this regard, software systems, such as Dynix, provide a template for community services information that can help with technical aspects of community information. For the most part, technical facilitators are available on most of the school campuses to help with technical problems as they arise and to offer technical advice with planning for new programs. Library media center web pages are now common in schools in the area and, in recent years, have generally become linked to public library web pages.

Professional Experiences

The question about the extent of professional experience with community information and responses helped to point out the flexible nature of community information. Most, if not all, of the participants had been involved with community information in some way, whether by formal or informal contacts with teachers, students, parents, and member of the community.

Information Literacy

In response to a question concerning whether information literacy was or can be incorporated in community information services, the group noted that in schools students are taught problem-solving skills so that they can go to sources on their own to find information. But community information may not necessarily be a part of the curriculum that is taught in classes.

Local Examples

The focus group was unable to point out only one local school example of an ongoing community service, the Austin Public Library's Wired for Youth program. In this program students are encouraged to talk to people in the community as a way of learning to better use electronic sources. Although not a part of a school media library program, the Connections Resource Center (http://www. connectionscenter.org/site/PageServer) was also noted as a source for community information closely associated with school and parenting needs.

Final Recommendations and Insights

The following is a summary of the major recommendations made by the group:

1. Information is only useful *when it's needed*;
2. Information must be offered in a number of different ways (e.g., e-mails, websites, vertical file, paper sources);
3. Contact and send information to community associations via e-mails and list services;
4. E-mail is now the vehicle of choice to provide information;
5. Offer a list of book titles on the school library web page;
6. List current issues and topics of concern to the public (e.g., "How to Cope with War") and link to the library catalog for further information;
7. Make sure that 311 services offered by police departments are clearly noted on the library's website. As 311 services often receive reference-type requests, 311 personnel need to be informed about how to make referrals to local libraries.

Responses from the Field Survey Groups

This assessment approach used a convenience sample of school and public librarians involved in a series of in-service workshops during the summer and fall of 2003. The workshops had nothing to do with community information, but they were used as a means of reaching diversified groups of librarians who worked with youth. These workshops were conducted in several regions of the United States including Kentucky, Missouri, Ohio, and Texas. Similar, if not identical, questions were asked of both the focus groups and the workshop participants. (See Appendix 3 for the survey questionnaire). Fifty-one librarians participated in this series of workshops by responding to a questionnaire asking questions relating to community information in school library media centers. Respondents consisted of eighteen school librarians (32%); thirty-eight public librarians (67%); and one special librarian (2%). Figures presented here reflect one response to specific questions. Not all librarians responded to all questions, and adjustments were made for responses that included more than one response per question when only one response was requested.

Defining Community

Most respondents in the groups considered community information as more of a state of mind than a community limited by geographic boundaries (N = 35, 63%). School librarians also agreed with this concept of community information (N = 10, 56%). These responses seemed to echo the feelings expressed by the focus group, reinforcing the idea that community is complex, and a purely geographic definition cannot account for the dynamic nature of community information within complex societies.

Meaning of Community Information

Most of the respondents tended to agree with Jones's definition of community information, (see Appendix 3), seeing it as a means of providing the individual user with information and assistance and directing the user to community sources where help can be obtained. School librarians in the survey either definitely agreed or generally agreed with this definition (N = 15, 83%). School librarians in the focus group tended to connect community information more with curriculum than did the public librarians in the focus group.

Community Information in the School Library Media Center

Thirty-six respondents (63%) felt that community information should be provided in the school library media center, while only five (9%) felt that it should not be provided. Interestingly, twelve (21%) had never considered the idea, and four (7%) were unsure. Sixty-one percent of school librarians agreed that community information belonged in a school library media program (N = 15), while three (11%) disagreed. Although this question was not presented directly to the focus group in this way, from overall responses, the focus group also agreed that community information should be a part of the school library center program.

Kinds of Community Information Materials to Be Provided

Given several choices and based on seventeen single responses, participants felt that the following three materials were the most important materials to be made available in a school library media center community information program. Twenty responses were not included because of multiple choices given. This in itself may indicate that community information is diverse and useful in many different formats. The following figures reflect only responses

from school library media center specialists and public librarians, with responses from the one special librarian in the survey being eliminated.

- Locally produced pamphlets, brochures, maps;
- Local links to community information on the Internet;
- Community bulletin boards for posting items.

School library media center specialists felt that a variety of community
information sources should be available in the school library media center
(N = 5, 45%). School librarians also felt that website links to local community information were important resources (N = 3, 27%). Materials considered less important by all respondents included local community information
files, closed-circuit community information television, locally produced directories, and vertical/information files. When compared separately, and
based on eleven responses, school librarians tended to feel that all types of
resources listed in the survey for consideration were important (N = 5, 45%).
In comparison, the focus group tended to consider information materials in
terms of curriculum support. Figure 6.2 illustrates how school and public
librarians and library media specialists in the survey considered selected types
of options for resources as appropriate for a school library media center program.

Strengths of Community Information Programs

Based on fifty-four responses, the survey group noted of three important
strengths of a school library media center program:

- Provides a useful information service;
- Helps students understand how to live in the world;
- Is helpful in promoting critical thinking and information literacy skills.

Figure 6.3 presents a comparison between school library media specialists
and public librarians regarding strengths of programs.
    Lesser noted strengths included its usefulness in promoting academic
achievement and learning and in its adding depth to curriculum. Only three
survey participants felt that community information programs had no
strengths in terms of the options presented in the survey. School media center
librarians in the survey agreed with those attributes as well. The focus group
again felt that curriculum needs would be well served by a community information program. In addition to curriculum, and as noted previously, they
especially felt that a community information program would enhance instructional support offered to teachers and promote parental involvement through
the sharing of skills and volunteer services.

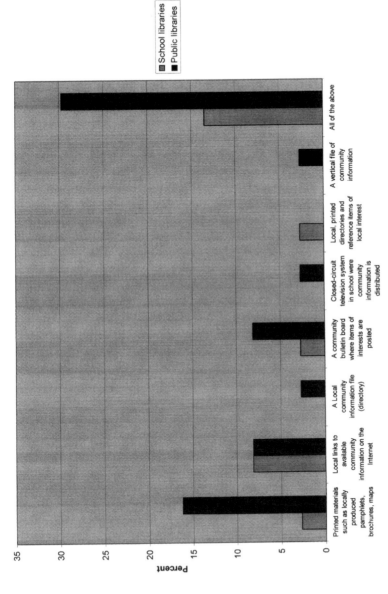

Figure 6.2 Services (Resources) for a School Library Media Center Community Information Program

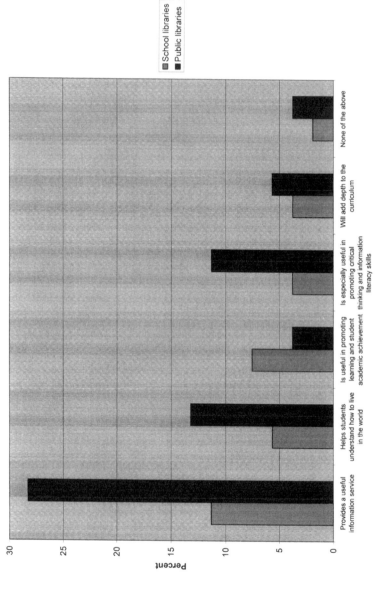

Figure 6.3 Strengths of a School Library Media Center Community Information Program

Problems Presented by Community Information Programs

In terms of problems, the survey group noted three major problem areas:

- Time consuming to establish and maintain;
- Schools would not have administrative support in my community;
- There is very little demand for it in most schools.

School library media specialists (based on eighteen responses) also agreed that offering the service was time consuming (N = 9, 50%), but they noted two other limitations, including little demand for the service (N = 2, 11%) and that the service does not promote the overall mission of the school (N = 2, 11%). Figure 6.4 provides a comparison between school library media specialists and public librarians relating to perceived problems. In addition, the focus group noted cost, insurance, liability, and staffing and security concerns as problems.

Skills Required

As with the focus group, some of the survey respondents felt that their library staff had the skills to maintain community information websites (N = 24, 42%), but 58% (N = 33) said no or were unsure. Based on eighteen responses, school library media specialists reflected this trend as well, with eleven (61%) saying that their staff did have such skills, and seventeen (30%) saying that they were not sure or had no way of knowing.

Involvement with Community Information Programs

Many in the survey group had never been associated with a school library media community information program (N = 40, 70%), nor did most of them know of any currently operating programs (N = 39, 87%). From eighteen responses, school library media center specialists showed this trend as well, with eleven (61%) saying that they had never been associated with a school having community information as a school media center service program. Seven (40%) noted that they had had such an association. Seventy-three percent (N = 11) of the school library media specialists could not recommend a current school-based community information program, while four (27%) indicated that they know of such programs. The lack of association with a school-based community information program was also true of the focus group. The focus group tended to identify community information sources within the community, not ones associated with schools.

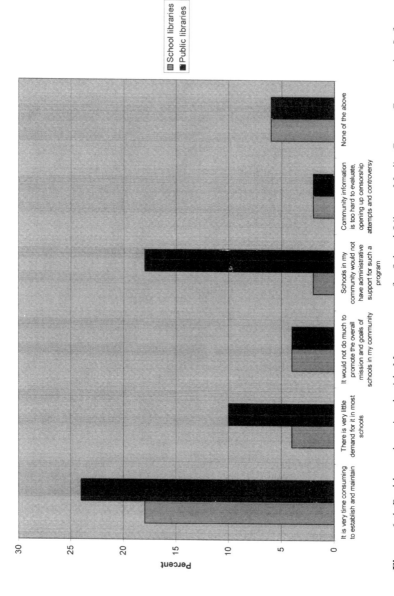

Figure 6.4 Problems Associated with Management of a School Library Media Center Community Information Program

Summary of Responses

Based on responses from both the focus and the survey groups, community information has baseline support. The data appear to support these factors:

- Community information is not identified by geographic boundaries, reinforcing its complexity for both personal and curriculum uses.
- It is perceived more as a collection and directive type of service than a counseling or advice-giving service.
- The most popular materials to include in school library media center collections are locally produced materials, such as bulletins, brochures, and maps. Much of this material might well be considered as giveaway items. Bulletin boards used for the posting of community information are also important. School library media specialists see community information resources as diversified.
- The strengths of a community information program relate to curriculum and teaching support, helping youth better understand their world, and promoting critical thinking skills. In addition, a community information program can help forge better links and communication with the wider community and with parents.
- Both the focus and the survey group felt that technical and administrative skills generally are available to support such programs, but there is a level of uncertainty here.
- Weaknesses of such programs include the time and expense of establishing and maintaining the program and a perceived lack of demand or need for such programs, as well as a lack of administrative support.
- Most of the respondents in the survey groups had little experience with or actual knowledge of active school library media center programs. Those few who did respond to the LM_NET inquiry had more experience with the concept and practice and had considered some of the management issues involved in providing community information. The interesting aspects of these responses indicate that a viable community information program can exist in a school library media center, aided tremendously by a well-managed website with links to appropriate sources from the community and the Internet.

Some of the problems presented in this survey and especially noted by the focus group relate directly to marketing and how to inform potential users about the value of community information. Awareness of community information is most important as it relates directly to providing useful information to both individual students and to offering support for student achievement and learning. Some of these marketing and information issues are discussed further in chapter 7.

LOCAL MODELS FOR CONSIDERATION

Several models are available for school library media center specialists to follow based on their individual circumstances. The models, as outlined here, reflect three stages of development: Stage 1: Basic, Stage 2: Midlevel, and Stage 3: Advanced.

Stage 1: Basic. The basic level concentrates on immediate community information sources found both in the school and in the immediate neighborhood. These resources may be clippings from local newspapers, pamphlets for distribution provided by local organizations, and local directories published in the area. A well-designed and well-maintained community information bulletin board needs to be provided where clippings and notices are systematically posted. A small information file may also be maintained where important items are filed after they are removed from the bulletin board. A small center for the distribution of free pamphlets may also be maintained, as well as a collection of directories for in-library consultation. At this level, the school library media specialist needs to be aware of professionals in both the school and local community where referrals based on school policies and procedures can be made. The staff may also want to begin a file of local persons who have collections and talents to share with students. Community information resources, critical uses, and evaluation should be a central part of the information literacy program.

Stage 2: Midlevel. In addition to those services, including information literacy, offered at the basic level, a midlevel service can offer links on its website to local community information, such as the local public library and other closely related community service groups. A graphic/pictures collection may also be feasible at this level. Electronic graphics of community information resources (e.g., local historic sites) may be created and uploaded to the local library web page. Photoprint and local information files with appropriate subject headings may also be maintained at this level.

Stage 3: Advanced. Building on elements found in stages 1 and 2, an advanced program will need to consider means of integrating local information into the school's online catalog. Advanced approaches to web page linage will also be needed at this level. In keeping with school policies and procedures, referral services will need to be extensively developed here. The more advanced programs will carefully consider the needs for an archival program, including the demands for reference services, preservation of materials, and the standard organization of the materials. Information literacy education should continue to emphasize the importance of community information in all its social and psychological contexts.

CRITICAL THINKING SKILLS AND COMMUNITY INFORMATION

Critical thinking and process-centered education are closely related to these recommendations from the field and to the previously mentioned three models in terms of information literacy education. Process-centered education emphasizes the importance of individual learning and how to develop skills regardless of the subject matter. In other words, process education is a unifying, holistic approach in learning and applying these principles no matter what the subject content. The mental processes involved include:

- Analysis
- Inference
- Classification (e.g., relationships and associations)
- Measurement (e.g., balance vs. completeness)

All these elements are necessary for students to use community information well.

In addition, critical thinking is embedded in process education. Critical thinking is reflective thinking that is focused on deciding what to do or to believe. Critical thinking has an important role in community information skills, as it teaches these important aspects of seeking information, no matter the subject domain.[11] How to:

- Ask questions and evaluate a situation;
- Evaluate information relating to the question at hand;
- Seek out information relating to the question;
- Evaluate the information—reject, accept, modify;
- Apply the information to the question at hand (abstract, synthesis, interpret);
- Create a product (paper, speech, solution, model).

Aside from formal, group-based instruction in community information, other methods of instruction are also appropriate. As mentioned by Brake, preparation of finding aids, bibliographies, and lists are necessary, as are instructions on how to use special tools unique to the school library media center and community. For example, the online catalog with its links to community information would likely have to be taught. Information instruction at point of need is effective. For example, if a student new to the neighborhood wanted to find out how to join a local sports league or youth activity center, instruction as to how to find the information in the community information system and how to make contact could be given when the question is first asked.

One of the most popular models for teaching information skills is the Big6 model developed by Mike Eisenberg and Bob Berkowitz. The developers claim that this is the world's most widely used school-based information instructional method. The model was undoubtedly influenced by Benjamin Blooms' taxonomy of learning as well as process-centered education.[12] The model also reflects process education in that it places emphasis on analysis, inference, classification, and measurement.[13] The Big6 approach has six components:

- Task Definition
  - Define the information problem.
  - Identify information needed in order to complete the task (to solve the information problem).
- Information-Seeking Strategies
  - Determine the range of possible sources (brainstorm).
  - Evaluate the different possible sources to determine priorities (select the best sources).
- Location and Access
  - Locate sources (intellectually and physically).
  - Find information within sources.
- Use of Information
  - Engage (e.g., read, hear, view, touch) the information in a source.
  - Extract relevant information from a source.
- Synthesis
  - Organize information from multiple sources.
  - Present the information.
- Evaluation (judge the product for effectiveness; judge the process for efficiency).

The model is fully explained on the website, http://big6.com.

Numerous guides are available to help school library media specialists plan an information literacy program adaptable for community information instruction. These include:

- Jane Birks and Fiona Hunt. *Hands-On Information Literacy Activities*. Neal-Schuman, 2000.
- Michael B. Eisenberg, Carrie A. Lowe, and Kathleen L. Spitzer. *Information Literacy: Essential Skills for the Information Age*, 2nd ed. Libraries Unlimited, 2004.
- Norma Heller. *Information Literacy and Technology Research Projects Grades 6–9*. Libraries Unlimited, 2001.
- Iowa City Community School District. *Developing an Information Literacy Program K–12: A How-to-Do-It Manual*. Edited by Mary Jo Langhorne. Neal-Schuman, 1998.
- Ellen Jay and Hilda L. Jay. *250+ Activities and Ideas for Developing Literary Skills*. Neal-Schuman, 1998.
- Ann Marlow Riedling. *Learning to Learn: A Guide to Becoming Information Literate*. Neal-Schuman, 2002.
- Nancy P. Thomas. *Information Literacy and Information Skills Instruction: Applying Research to Practice in the School Library Media Center*. Edited by Paula Kay Montgomery. Libraries Unlimited, 1999.

Site management is another way of providing direction to community information. Adequate and psychologically supportive sign systems, floor plans, logical placement of community information resources, and, of course, readily available help and information desks are necessary for a complete instruction system.

RELATED STUDIES AND PROGRAMS HELPFUL IN PLANNING COMMUNITY INFORMATION SERVICES

Related studies concerning the information needs of youth are likewise helpful in determining the focus of a local community information program. A few of these are briefly described here. For example, consumer health information is intended for use by laypersons and not necessarily by medical professionals. It is intended to help the lay public understand health issues and take an active part in their own health care. A number of studies in the 1990s showed that the information needs of youth are rather consistent and that they are concerned about a number of issues, including HIV-AIDS, education opportunities, race relations, violence, rape, teen suicide, guns, homosexuality, premarital sex and relationships, body building and personal attractiveness, abortion, child abuse, the environment, drinking and driving, drugs and drug abuse, the economy, sex information, birth control, relationships, and entertainment.

Based on survey data, the "Bay Area Youth-at-Risk Project," sponsored by a number of public libraries in the Bay Area of California, decided to develop a number of service models that would better serve at-risk youth. Among other recommendations, these models called for procedures that would[14]

- Provide basic information about community services;
- Improve the young adult collection;
- Develop special programs and services for youth, especially in the areas of job information, multicultural issues, health and sex information, and poetry as political expression (rap music and poetry);
- Offer tutoring programs;
- Maintain community outreach services (visits to tutoring centers, juvenile halls, school and parenting programs);
- Integrate youth into the planning process of the library.

The Memphis/Shelby County Public Library and Information Center has been particularly innovative in developing community information programs. In the 1980s, the library mounted an intense HIV-AIDS program directed toward the at-risk population. They met with gay and lesbian social and political groups in the city and encouraged them to support the use of the library for HIV-AIDS information. The library contacted government agencies and cooperated with them in offering various programs and services; they prepared and offered training materials about information sources to various groups in Spanish; they provided a document delivery service to agencies for materials found in the National Library of Medicine's AIDS database; they produced television programs for local cable broadcasting; and they produced reading lists and reference guides for the general public. The library also developed "Joblinc Service."

This service lists jobs, locates training opportunities, and helps with one-on-one searches and preparing for interviews. Joblinc is closely tied to the library's community information service and online human service directory. This is a mobile service that allows the program to function in various neighborhoods where unemployment is high. Joblinc and other current services offered by the library are described at http://www.memphislibrary.org/toc/lsercol.htm.

The Baltimore County Public Library Program

In the early 1970s in Maryland, the Baltimore County Public Library initiated a survey of secondary school students in both public and private schools in Baltimore County to determine what they needed and wanted in the way of information, with emphasis on community information. Results of this program were reported in an early publication called *Connections*.[15] Since then, the program has expanded and now includes a web page on the library's website at http://www.bcplonline.org/commpg/connections. The library's page describes the site as follows:

> In Baltimore County, there are many community organizations with trained staff to answer questions and help find the information needed to make informed decisions. "The Connections: Children, Youth and Family Resources Directory" is a listing of those organizations that work with children, youth and their families. Connections has been designed to help you make a direct connection with the organization that can provide the most appropriate services for you. We hope you will find the directory a useful self-help guide to the many services available in our County.

"Connections" includes entries for government agencies at the federal, state, local, county, and city levels, as well as non-profit organizations. Businesses are included only if they offer services that are difficult for consumers to locate. Businesses that are readily found in the yellow pages of phone directories or those who advertise their services widely are not included. Selection of organizations for inclusion in the directory is reviewed by the Connections Editorial Board of the Baltimore County Children and Youth Council. A print version of the directory was published in 1997.[16]

INFOhio (Ohio) and Boone County Schools (Kentucky)

INFOhio (http://www.infohio.org) is "state-funded resources free to all Ohio's K-12 students and teachers." In most respects, it is similar to other systems, such as the now defunct Texas Library Connection (TLC). What may be somewhat different about this system is that it does provide carefully selected links to community information that are directly related to school activities and curriculum needs, such as art museums. It also links directly to the Ohio Public Library Information Network, which offers a broader approach to community resources. A search of the website showed that it appears to avoid posted links to controversial issues, such as sexuality.

The Boone County Schools (http://www.boone.k12.ky.us/), located in Florence in Northern Kentucky, offers an impressive website of information related to the needs of staff, teachers, parents, and students. Its many links offer a wide array of information, much of which is apparently available to anyone who logs onto the site. One of its links, "Infoplease," a commercial database owned by Disney, is rich in information, as it offers a variety of informational sources, including an almanac, an atlas, a dictionary, and encyclopedias, as well as information especially created for teachers, parents, and students. It links to Kentucy's KYVirtual Library and its various components, including library catalogs (http://www.kyvl.org). However, some of its links require passwords. On the whole, local community information, as defined in this book, does not appear to be offered on the Boone County Schools site or through KYVirtual Library.

MODELS AND PROGRAMS HELPFUL TO SCHOOL LIBRARY MEDIA CENTERS

Although many of the programs previously described are public library programs, they present significant directions for organization and management and offer ideas for cooperation with school libraries in terms of community information. The school sites discussed are also of value because they present frameworks that can easily accommodate local community information.

As Brake pointed out years ago, schools and other agencies, especially the public library, have an important cooperative role to play in providing better access to community information for students. Programs such as those by the Bay Area Librarians, the Baltimore County Public Library, and the Memphis and Shelby County public libraries that offer strong outreach programs are natural allies for school libraries in developing community information services. School library media center programs need not exist in isolation in terms of community information.

SELECTED ISSUES AND PROBLEMS

In addition to issues and problems discussed in this and previous chapters, such as selection and use, censorship and government control, sources of community information and how to acquire and organize them, and networking, other problems and issues remain.

Readability, Concept, and Design Issues

Readability and concept issues are present in all aspects of community information. In addition to design features, websites must be developed so that sites are both readable and age-appropriate in terms of vocabulary and conceptual development. This is true of all computer-based information sources. A 1997 study reported that the readability levels of health information found in the Health Information Center on InfoTrac exceeded the eighth-grade reading level, indicating that it would not be usable for persons with poor reading skills.[17] Readability and conceptual appropriateness also affects handout materials, materials posted on community bulletin boards, displays of materials, and other aspects of community information. For example, reading level and conceptual level studies of pamphlets and brochures designed to give basic consumer health information to low-education-level persons have been found to be too advanced in concepts and reading levels to be of much benefit. A 1975 study found that of nine brochures distributed at a mental health clinic in the Chicago area, only one could be read at the sixth-grade level, with four of these nine pamphlets requiring a college-level reading ability.[18] The same might be said of displays and bulletin boards. A later study by Hans H. Johnson and his associates suggested that similar health pamphlets and brochures be written at readability levels no lower than grade 5.0 and no higher than grade 5.9.[19]

Consideration must be given to conceptual development of the audience in terms of the information as well as the reading levels of materials posted and displayed. Depending on the age and development level of the audience, along with written words, displays and bulletin boards will often require the use of visuals and graphics to fully convey the scope and breadth of the information provided. Elizabeth Szudy and Michele Arroyo recommend that materials for persons with limited literacy skills be written so that they can be easily read, that they be visually designed so that they are appealing, and that they use graphics in instructive ways to explain concepts found in texts.[20] Regarding these concepts, community information materials need to follow the same section criteria as other library materials.

Sensitive Community Information

Because community information includes a wide variety of information reflecting the life, interests, and activities found in the community, sensitive issues and content can be expected. In practical application, this really is no different in concept than materials that are acquired for the school media library collection. As has been stated previously in this book, community information and its acquisition and dissemination must be based on well-developed and legally defensible selection and acquisition policies just as a selection policy guides the acquisition of book and nonbook materials.

Sex and sexuality, health information, and mental health concerns are sensitive topics of particular concern. Following official selection policies, such information can be acquired based on age-appropriateness, curriculum needs, information needs, and personal development needs of students. Built into the selection policy can be statements that especially address the types of community information that are systematically acquired. Special procedures can be included in the selection policy, such as having professional-level selection committees approve all websites that are mounted on the school library media center's website. To avoid the idea that this committee is a censoring committee, the selection policy must carefully explain the role of the committee and how it adheres to principles of free access to information and the rights of youth to information. A review process used by the Baltimore County Public Library (BCPL) is one to consider. BCPL uses a professional committee representing several social services and educational agencies in the county to review and approve all links added to its Youth page. Other credible websites and community networks exist through the United States, Canada, Great Britain, and other countries that offer appropriate resources for local community information services.

Censorship Concerns

Lester Asheim, in his classic explanation of selection of materials as opposed to censorship of materials, defined selection as a positive approach, in that it, as a process, "[seeks] value in the book as a book and in books as a while." Censorship, on the other hand, is negative in that it seeks vulnerable characteristics in a book or item wherever they may be found—in the book or item as well as external to it. He also considered selection to be a process that protects the reader's ability to read and to have access to information. On the other hand, censorship seeks to protect the reader or information user from the harmful effects of reading or information. Selection affirms and frees the reader while censorship controls the reader. Asheim affirms that American democratic society has also placed its value with the selector rather than the censor.[21]

The right to control information and to censor in some fashion or another is practiced by most governments. Justifications for such censorship are based on moral, religious, or national security needs, and such practices are often reinforced by legislative laws and court interpretations of law. In the United States, the U.S. Constitution and its First Amendment are central to how censorship is or is not practiced. The U.S. Constitution is a rigid document in that it cannot be changed easily by the enactment of laws and government policies. All laws, regulations, ordinances, orders, and other acts performed or passed by governments at all levels must conform to the Constitution.

The Constitution and courts' interpretations of the Constitution in rela-
tion to the rights of youth for information and access to materials in school
library media collections have varied over the years, but, today, the primary
court interpretation is found in *Board of Education, Island Trees, New York
vs. Pico* (457 U.S. 853). Although the court recognized the important role
of local school boards to establish and direct curriculum and to maintain a
suitable atmosphere for learning, it also recognized the rights of students to
information found in school library media collections. According to Tyll van
Geel, the court ruled that students have an "inherent corollary of rights of
free speech and press and can receive information in a variety of contexts,"
and materials cannot be removed from school library media collections based
on ideological content that might be objectionable to members of a board.[22]
The Supreme Court reasoned that school boards may remove books based
on sound educational reasons and that these reasons are open to public scrutiny, and removals must be able to withstand challenges in courts. For example, a district court declared that a school board in Kansas had removed
Annie on My Mind in violation of the Constitution (*Case v. Unified School
District* No. 233, 908 F. Supp. 864, 1995). This court rejected the board's
argument saying that the board had based its interpretation of education
soundness to mean anything other than its own agreements and wrote that
there was "viewpoint discrimination" in the board's decision to remove the
book.[23] In 2003, a U.S. district judge in Arkansas ordered the popular Harry
Potter books returned to school library shelves in the Cedarville school district. His order read that these books must be housed "where they can be
accessed without any restrictions other than those administrative restrictions
that apply to all works of fiction in the libraries of the district."[24] The court
reasoned further that:

> "the stigmatizing effect of having to have parental permission to check out a
> book constitutes a restriction on access," one which has been significantly lim-
> ited by U.S. Supreme Court decisions that "stress the importance of freedom
> of speech in the education of America's youth" and recognize that a school li-
> brary is an "environment especially appropriate for the recognition of the First
> Amendment rights of students."[25]

From such decisions, it is clear that when censorship challenges reach
courts, motives of boards in removing books from school library media collections are seriously considered. In recent years, courts have often used
Pico to help determine the constitutionality of laws and policies involving
information disseminated through the Internet in public libraries. Implied
in *Pico* is the right of youth to receive information and to learn. Although
the Court ruled only on books, by extension, the principles in this ruling
can easily apply to community information disseminated by school library
media centers.

Access to Community Information and Government Control

In the United States, school and public libraries are under government scrutiny to see that they do not offer youth inappropriate information found on the Internet. This scrutiny is now found in law and court rulings that have affected access to Internet information at the local level. Especially in responses to the *Children's Internet Protection Act* (CIPA), school libraries across the country have enacted strict access rules regarding what is available to students. Some schools employ commercial filter programs, while others have left selection in the hands of selected school officials. This sometimes has included library media specialists and other staff members who have information expertise. Sometimes filtering decisions are out of the hands of the library media specialists entirely, while in other situations library media specialists can appeal decisions to filter a certain site. Whatever the local procedures, information from the Internet will need to conform to local school policies, legal mandates, and court decisions regarding legislative actions.

Access to Information and the Rise of Terrorism

Access to information and the right to have that access protected are involved here as well. As stated previously, school library media specialists as well as other librarians must abide by law, but they should also be aware of the impact on privacy of laws such as the USA PATRIOT Act and must be able to explain how such acts have the potential for eroding the concept of privacy of information use. Among other provisions, this Act allows FBI agents to search library records without "probable cause" to acquire records of anyone they believe to have information relevant to a terrorism investigation, "including people who are not suspected of committing a crime or of having any knowledge of a crime." Requests for such searches are heard by a secret court in closed proceedings that makes it impossible for "librarians to have the opportunity to object on First Amendment grounds prior to the execution of the order." The order also contains a "gag provision" that prevents librarians from informing anyone that a search of records has occurred. Even after the fact, based on this law, librarians could not protest the search.[26]

Recognizing the problems that this Act holds for First Amendment rights, Representative Bernie Sanders of Vermont in March 2003 introduced House Bill 1157, "Freedom to Read Protection Act of 2003" (H.R. 1157). This act "strengthens protections for the privacy of bookstore and library records." According to the Act, law enforcement officials are still able to "subpoena bookstore and library records crucial to an investigation, but the courts will exercise their normal scrutiny in reviewing these requests."[27] Still concerned with the effects of the PATRIOT Act on freedom of expression and the access to information in 2004, the American Library Association along with other groups launched a petition drive to restore privacy safeguards to the USA PATRIOT Act.[28]

Privacy and Confidentiality

Aside from the provisions of the PATRIOT Act, because of the variety of community information resources that relate directly to personal needs and situations, privacy and confidentiality must be respected. Libraries and school library media specialists have long respected the right of circulation records to remain private and available to others only on a court order. Similarly, sensitive reference questions have remained confidential. Adherence to such policies and procedures are extremely important regarding community information of a personal nature. School media specialists need to be mindful that privacy must be allowed for searching the Internet as well as searching and asking questions of the staff. Often this can be achieved by simple arrangement of furniture, which provides a sense of privacy. Figure 6.5 shows how furniture can be arranged to provide for good traffic flow and supervision while at the same time ensuring a sense of privacy.

Computer terminals and carrels can also be arranged so that a person using a terminal is provided with a sense of privacy. This can be achieved by placing terminals away from heavy traffic areas and by making sure that the ar-

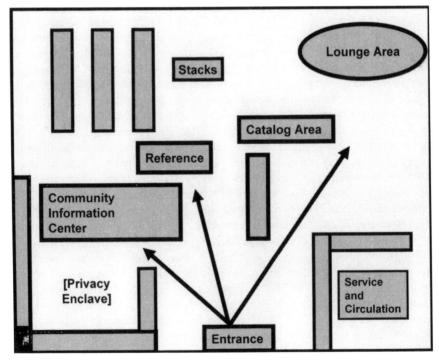

Figure 6.5 Furnishings, Traffic Patterns, and Privacy

rangement of the terminals does not encourage lines to form around persons using the terminals. Computer terminals should be arranged so that privacy is maintained while also allowing for needed supervision and assistance. Similarly, carrels often are designed with privacy in mind. They too can be arranged so that a sense of privacy is assured. Because of privacy often associated with the Internet and filtering issues, some libraries are now acquiring computer carrels that have the screens recessed below the surface, preventing or discouraging others from viewing screen images.

Dedicated terminals for community information may also ensure a sense of privacy. Figure 6.6 illustrates these concepts.

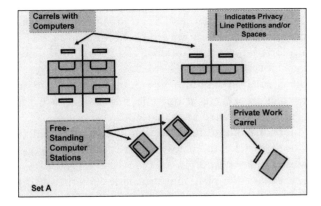

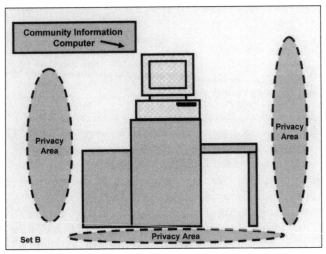

Figure 6.6 Dedicated Computer Terminal Stations and Placement of Carrels for Privacy

The reference desk should also be arranged so that privacy is maintained. This is best accomplished by having the desk away from the circulation area and by promoting a one-on-one relationship with the information specialist and the client. The arrangement of desks and chairs can suggest privacy and can prevent others from intruding on a conversation between user and media specialist. This is more difficult to maintain when reference questions are answered at a counter. Counters at reference points do not allow for much privacy as people tend to line up for service. A much better way to afford privacy is to have an office-like appearance where the information specialist is seated at a desk and a chair is provided for persons interacting with the specialist. This sends a nonverbal message that this is a private conversation, and most people will allow for some degree of personal space between them and the persons in the conference situation.

Encounters at the circulation desk are frequent and the arrangement of this important unit can go a long way in promoting privacy. The circulation desk should not be compact and cluttered and should provide enough space so that one can move to a more private area for an involved conversation. Notice that the circulation desk in Figure 6.7 is arranged so that the normal activities of circulation remains at one end of the desk, while more private conversation can be conducted at the far end.

Places for individual study and reflection are likewise needed. The traditional library study carrel with enclosed sides is excellent for this, and commercial firms offer many selections.

Useful resources for the planning of facilities conducive to private consultation include:

- Steven Baule. *Facilities Planning for School Library Media & Technology Centers.* Linworth, 1999.
- Thomas L. Hart. *The School Library Media Facilities Planner.* Neal-Schuman, 2004.

Counseling Concepts and Applications

One of the hallmarks of community information is the need for advice and counseling associated with information requests and needs. Often such information requests are emotional, as they impact a person's life. Public libraries have generally avoided giving advice in their role as providers of community information. However, the Public Library Association has recognized the importance of this and has advised librarians when providing community information that they must be prepared to attend to the emotional needs of those seeking information.[29] On the whole, public libraries have remained content to offer what has been called "simple information and referral" services. This consists of obtaining the necessary information and providing access to it through websites, directories, and other avenues of dissemina-

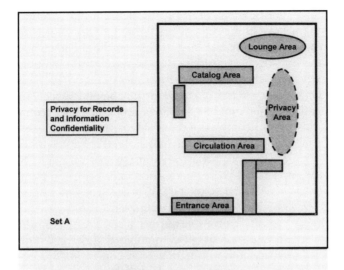

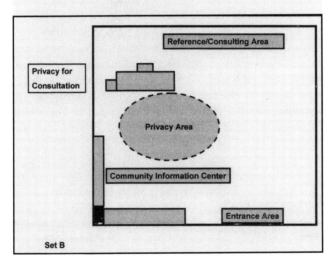

Figure 6.7 Circulation and Reference Desk Placement for Consultation and Privacy

tion; receiving a request for information and searching the files for the information using both internal and external files; and giving the information found in this search to the client. This often includes directing the client to organizations or other outlets where service and advice can be obtained. More complex information and referral consists of detailed questioning of the client, assessment of the client needs, placing needs into priority, negotiating with the client in terms of needs, and then giving the client detailed and personalized information based on his or her needs. Complex referral means that the agent assumes an advocacy role for the client by contacting resources, making appointments, negotiating on the client's behalf, making sure that the client's rights to services are honored, and obtaining recourse to third parties if the client's needs are not met.[30]

As information and referral moves into the complex aspects of information giving and referral, counseling skills become more needed and important. It is at this level of complexity that many public librarians by definition and practice have not moved. Nevertheless, several major public libraries (Atlanta, Cleveland, Detroit, Houston, and Queens Borough, New York) involved in the important Urban Neighborhood Information Center Project used various levels of social workers and other types of case workers in facilitating their community information programs.[31]

Over the years, library education has been criticized because of its perceived failure to educate students in communication. If these criticisms are true, they would impact on how librarians view community information and service. In 1974, library educator Helen Gothberg wrote that librarians have difficulty in understanding that people need help in asking for information, and they have difficulty in giving counseling support when needed. She also holds that librarians generally do not understand that people need help in understanding the information that they have at hand. Because of their traditionally passive role, Gothberg also noted that librarians do not know how to motivate people to participate in their quest for information and to learn from their experiences with libraries and information.[32] These behaviors are all aspects of counseling that Goldberg suggested are necessary for effective library and information work with clients.

Counseling and communication skills are not new to librarians. Evidence of this is found in literature of librarians well back into the nineteenth century.[33] One of the most interesting examples of counseling is the concept reported by David K. Maxfield in which he described how the reference department of the University of Illinois at Chicago was turned into the Department of Library Instruction and Advisement. In this new department, the staff performed conventional reference work, gave library instruction, and offered reader's advisement. At the same time, they served at the "sub-clinical level" in assisting the counselors with advisement and guidance, and making suitable referrals. The librarians were particularly involved with vocational, educational advisement, and, to some degree, in personal adjustment where they selected and organized materials and acted as a liaison between the library and the counseling center.[34]

In their understanding of counseling, both Maxfield and Penland agreed that counseling is more involved than answering reference questions or providing reading advisement. When librarians move into counselor roles they, like other counselors, help their clients focus and develop plans for solving problems. In encouraging this level of problem solving, Penland suggest that librarians go well beyond the use of resources found in their libraries and involve the client with a variety of resources, including community resources. Penland's idea of the counselor librarian is one where the librarian attempts to help the clients grow and improve by listening to them and by encouraging them to understand the nature of their problems and to plan strategies for dealing with those problems. Although the retrieval of information is important, Penland maintains that the counselor librarians seek to change behavior in positive ways and to recognize the importance of personal growth and development and, through their actions, to influence that growth and development.[35]

Associated with counseling is the concept of the helping relationship. Writing in 1978, public librarian Lethene Parks explained how the helping relationship was very much a part of librarianship.[36] She drew upon humanist psychologist Carl Rogers's definition of the helping process as a relationship in which helpers are "intent on promoting the growth, development, maturity, improved functioning, and improved coping with life" of those they help.[37]

Social work educators Joseph Devitis and John Rich say that professions construct various models of helping based on their philosophical and theoretical understandings of their roles in society. Whatever the context of the helping situation—homes, community agencies, classrooms—a helping profession seeks to improve the lives of others in line with its professional goals and objectives.[38] The school library media center specialist may not be a psychologist, but he or she is indeed a helper within the contextual role as defined by the profession. Like other helping professions, the school library media specialist interacts with clients, gathers data, helps make decisions, and intervenes when appropriate to help individuals and groups.[39]

A "helper" in a helping profession is "anyone who is deemed by society as a person that should be helping other people to improve and grow." Many processes are involved in the helping relationship, including counseling, teaching, guiding, training, and educating. The helping persons involved in these processes, including librarians, are trying to influence others by their programs, services, and interventions, and thereby change behaviors in positive ways so that change and growth can take place.[40]

The relationship of these concepts to community information is clear. Community information involves many aspects of life and living; it is gathered from the community and reflects the interests, concerns, and resources of the community. Its use requires more than organization and dissemination; a connection must be made between the information, the community, and the user and his or her personal needs and wants. Appropriate use of counseling skills, communication skills, and helping behaviors can bring library users and community together in meaningful and powerful ways. The classic work by the late Naomi Brill and Joanne Levine, *Working with People: The Helping Process*, is an excellent guide for all professionals who help and guide people in all types of environments.[41]

School library media specialists play an important role in these endeavors. Their role has always involved some level of counseling and the use of helping skills. Their role as information and materials consultants and advisers to teachers, administrators, staff, students, and parents in the wise use of information is strong testimony to the importance of the school library media center to both the overall mission and objective of the school and its curriculum and to the community life of any school community.

CONCLUSION

Numerous models exist of how community information can be used in schools. As mentioned, many of these came from public libraries. Nevertheless, the experience afforded by the public library offers valuable guidance to school library media center specialists. Although published many years ago, the Brake study of how a community information center can be established in a school library is still a viable model worthy of review. Issues and problems do exist, and each school will find that it must develop its own way of providing community information. Nevertheless, it is an idea whose time has arrived.

NOTES

1. Risha W. Levinson, *New Routes to Human Services: Information and Referral* (New York: Springer, 2002), 24–35, 173.

2. Ibid., 28–29.

3. Ibid., 29.

4. Thomas Childers, *Third Year Continuation of a [Program to] Research and Design Criteria for the Implementation and Establishment of a Neighborhood Information Center in Five Public Libraries: Atlanta, Cleveland, Detroit, Houston, and Queens Borough*. Final Report (Washington, D.C.: U. S. Dept. of Health, Education, and Welfare, Office of Libraries and Learning Resources, 1975).

5. Thomas Childers, *Information and Referral: Public Libraries* (Norwood, N.J.: Ablex, 1984).

6. Ibid., 57.

7. Terence Brake, *The Need to Know: Teaching the Importance of Information*. Final Report for the Period January 1978–March 1979. (London: British Library, 1980), 3.

8. Ibid., 1–44.

9. Ibid., 45.

10. Clara S. Jones, ed., *Public Library Information and Referral Service* (Syracuse, N.Y.: Gaylord, 1978), 29.

11. Jerry D. Flack, *Mystery and Detection: Thinking and Problem Solving with the*

Sleuths (Englewood, Colo.: Teacher Ideas Press, 1990); JoAnn Vergona Krapp, "Teaching Research Skills: A Critical Thinking Approach," *School Library Journal* 34 (January 1988): 32–35.

12. Benjamin S. Bloom, ed., *Taxonomy of Educational Objectives: The Classification of Educational Goals*, by a Committee of College and University Examiners (and others), 1st ed. (New York, Longmans, Green, 1956).

13. Gene. R. Hawes and Lynne Salop Hawes Hawes, *The Concise Dictionary of Education* (New York: Van Nostrand Reinhold, 1982), 175.

14. Stan Weisner, *Information Is Empowering: Developing Public Library Services for Youth at Risk*. Bay Area Youth at Risk Project, ed. Katie Scarborough, 2nd ed. (Oakland, Calif.: Bay Area Library and Information System), 1992.

15. Baltimore County Public Library, *Connections: A Youth Service Directory* (Towson, Md.: The Library, ca. 1977).

16. *Connections: Children, Youth, & Family Resources*. An Interagency Cooperative Project of the Baltimore County Children and Youth Council, Baltimore County Department of Recreation and Parks, Baltimore County Public Library, Baltimore County Public Schools (Towson, Md.: The Library, 1997).

17. Lynda M. Baker, and others, "The Readability of Medical Information on InfoTrac: Does It Meet the Needs of People with Low Literacy Skills?" *Reference & User Services Quarterly* 37 (Winter 1997): 155–60.

18. Dale A. Brounstein and Homer H. Johnson, "Readability of Community Health Center Brochures for Client Consumption," *Journal of Community Psychology* 3 (April 1975): 193–95.

19. Hans H. Johnson and others, *Readability Study of Client Education Materials: A Resource for Assuring the Effectiveness of Written Materials*" (Raleigh, N.C.: North Carolina State Department of Environment, and Natural Resources, 1994). ERIC Reproduction No. ED 382 934.

20. Elizabeth Szudy and Michele Gonzalez Arroyo, *The Right to Understand: Linking Literacy to Health and Safety Training* (Berkeley, Calif.: University of California, Labor Occupation Program, 1994).

21. Lester Asheim, "Not Censorship but Selection," *Wilson Library Journal* 28 (September 1953): 63–67.

22. Tyll van Geel, "The Search for Constitutional Limits on Government Authority to Inculcate Youth," *Texas Law Review* 62 (October 1983): 197–297.

23. "Recent Cases, Briefly Noted: Removal of Book from Library," *Entertainment Law Reporter* 18 (August 1996), available at Lexis-Nexis Academic Universe, Legal Search, http://web.lesix-nexis.com/universe/documents?.

24. "Judge Blocks Censorship of Harry Potter Books in Arkansas Schools," *Free Expression Network*. Available at http://www.freexpression.org/newswire/0423_2003.htm.

25. "Justice, Not Magic, Returns Harry Potter Series to Library Bookshelves," *Legal Issues—Legal Update*, Center for Individual Freedom. Available at http://www.cfif.org/htdocs/legal_issues/legal_updates/first_amendment_cases/harry_potter.htm.

26. "Book and Library Community Supporting the Freedom to Read Act" (H.R. 1157), Free Expression Network. Available at http://www.freeexpression.org/ftrpa.htm.

27. Ibid.

29. "Book, Library Groups Launch Petition Drive to Restore Privacy Safeguards to USA Patriot Act." Available at http://www.freeexpression.org/newswire/0217_2004.htm.

30. Public Library Association, *Guidelines for Establishing Community Information and Referral Services in Public Libraries,* 4th ed. (Chicago: American Library Association, 1997).

31. Naomi I. Brill, *Working with People: The Helping Process* (New York: Longman, 1998), 212–16.

32. Childers, *Information and Referral: Public Libraries.*

33. Helen Gothberg, "Communication Patterns in Library Reference and Information Service," *RQ* 13 (Fall 1973): 7–14.

34. W. Bernard Lukenbill, "The Counselor Librarian: Fad or New Role for Youth Librarians," *Top of the News* 40 (Fall 1983): 81–82, citing Patrick Penland, "Counselor Librarians," in *Encyclopedia of Library and Information Science* (New York: Marcel Dekker, 1971), 241–42.

35. David K. Maxfield, *Counselor Librarianship: A New Departure.* Occasional Papers, no. 38 (Urbana: University of Illinois Library School, 1954).

36. Lukenbill, citing Maxfield and Penland.

37. Lethene Parks, "Research in Action: User-Oriented Service: The Librarian as Helper" *Public Libraries* 17 (Winter 1978): 14–15.

38. Parks, citing Carl Rogers, "The Characteristics of a Helping Relationship," in Donald L. Avila and others, eds., *The Helping Relationship Sourcebook* (Boston: Allyn & Bacon, 1971), 2–3.

39. Joseph L. DeVitis and John Martin Rich, *Helping and Intervention: Comparative Perspectives on the Impossible Professions* (New York: Irvington, 1988), 5–6.

40. Ibid.

41. Syllabus and Printed Lectures, Institute for Library Educators, "Interpersonal Communication, Adult Services, and Change" [*Higher Education Act*, Title II-B sponsored institute], June 10–30, 1974, Green Bay, Wisconsin.

42. Naomi I. Brill and Joanne Levine, *Working with People: The Helping Process,* 7th ed. (Boston: Allyn & Bacon, 2002).

CHAPTER 7

Marketing the Community Information Program

INTRODUCTION

This chapter discusses the general concept of marketing as it can be applied to community information within a school setting. Included in this discussion are general principles of marketing, such as basic definitions, approaches, and strategies. As discussed previously, workable models and procedures are important and necessary for the overall success of community information programs, but for a community information service to be a powerful force in the school, it must be marketed and sold to potential users in an effective manner.

WHAT IS MARKETING?

Marketing is essentially a selling process.[1] This includes developing a salable product, pricing it, promoting it, and distributing it to likely customers. Information presented in this chapter comes largely from Gilbert A. Churchill and J. Paul Peter's book *Marketing: Creating Value for Customers.*[2] The subtitle, *Creating Value for Customers*, is particularly relevant in the marketing of community information in school library media centers.

Like all marketing strategies,[3] marketing of a community information service must be based on the overall mission and goals of the school and of the school library media center. In other words, community information and the marketing of it must first and foremost exist within the framework of the parent institution—the school and its library media center program. A community information program in the school is informed by and answers to the curriculum and social and cultural objectives of the school.

Like all marketing strategies, marketing of a community information program will often require that a need for the product or service be developed. This is important when a concept is new and untried, as is often the case with community information within a school library media program. This is especially true when the service or product will be useful and of value to the customer or user. In this case, the marketing strategy is simply to provide information and to describe the usefulness of the service, thus allowing the potential user the choice of using the service. Through public relations campaigns, libraries of all types have sought to inform the public about their services and programs and to reinforce libraries and library programs as positive and rewarding for both the user and society in general. For example, in creating a desire for community information in the school, marketing strategies can provide information about the service, inform users about its value to them personally, and reinforce the importance of the library media center in the school as a central place for information and for curriculum support. Based on responses to questions in the survey discussed in chapter 6, informing potential users, and thereby creating a desire for the service, is extremely important because community information within a school library media center environment is still a new concept to most librarians.

STAGES OF MARKETING AND THEIR MEANINGS

In practical terms, marketing begins with a marketing plan. A marketing plan consists of several elements,[4] which include:

- Setting objectives for the marketing program;
- Identifying the target audience;
- Developing a marketing mix to serve each segment of the target audience.

Objectives of the marketing program are specific aims and accomplishments to which the marketing strategies and programs are directed. In the case of the school library media center, the *target audience* is a selected portion of a larger market group that a school library media center is attempting to serve. Said another way, a general market is made up of many different members, all of whom have different needs. A target audience is, therefore, a portion of this larger market that the library media center has decided to serve and includes students, teachers, administrators, staff members, and parents. The target market in a marketing plan can include one or several of these market elements.

Another term used in marketing is *marketing mix.* Marketing mix consists of controllable marketing variables that firms can use to generate profit through the sale of goods and services. For-profit firms use these variables to bring about the desired level of sales in their target markets. These variables consist of four elements:[5]

- Product;
- Pricing;
- Channel of distribution or placing the product in the market;
- Communication or promotion.

The Product

The product consists of goods or services that an organization offers to its target market, such as a community information service. The product also refers to the ways in which the goods and services have been enhanced to appeal to the target audience. In order to enhance the product, a product strategy needs to be developed. In commercial terms, the product strategy is development and design of the product, its packaging, and its positioning in the marketplace.

Pricing

Pricing is the element of the marketing mix that consists of setting prices that support the firm's organization marketing strategy. Not-for-profit organizations, such as school library media centers, set prices, but they do it in a different way than for-profit firms. They generally calculate the cost of the service and offer the service based on need and on how the organization can support the service through internal budget and staff support. Sometimes in not-for-profit organizations, the cost of the service is charged directly to the consumer, such as copying services or interlibrary costs.[6] Sometimes organizations such as libraries and museums may even offer merchandise for sale that promotes their cause. Price also includes the cost to the customer to acquire the product or service. Market experts Kotler, Roberto, and Lee offer these factors in terms of determining pricing:[7]

- Time, effort, and energy required to perform the behavior or acquire the product or service;
- Psychological risks and losses that the client might perceive or experiences in obtaining the product or service;
- The physical discomfort of changing behaviors or receiving the products or services.

In addition, convenience or the lack of convenience involved in obtaining the services or products is also a cost factor. As with marketing in gen-

eral, if the cost of the service or product is too high for the prospective customer, the service or product will not be acquired nor the desired behaviors
adopted.[8]

Channel of Distribution or Placing the Product in the Market

Placement and distribution of the product in a market is getting the product to the target audience so that it can be bought or used. Distribution is
critical in marketing. No matter how valuable the product is, members of
the target market will not buy it or use it if it is not readily available to them.
Accessibility and convenience of use are important aspects of product placement, and this concept is very important for school library media specialists
to consider in developing a marketing strategy for community information.

Communication, Promotion, and Advertising

Communication or promotion is part of the market mix and it is the process of informing the target audience about the organization and its products. Businesses use several means to communicate and promote their
products and services. These include:[9]

- Advertising;
- Personal selling;
- Sales promotions and incentives;
- Publicity and public relations;
- Design of messages;
- Communication design;
- Atmospherics.

In marketing, *advertising* is considered paid, nonpersonal communication
using various media to promote name identification with products and services in attempts to inform and persuade a given market to use or buy particular products or services.[10] With some exceptions, libraries rarely advertise
because of traditions and the cost involved.

Personal Selling, Sales Promotions, and Incentives

Personal selling is the direct interaction between the salesperson and the
customer. This is a common practice in the school library media center, where
media specialists are often involved in promoting reading and information
use through personal communication.[11] *Sales promotions* involve various
media approaches and are meant to alert a given market about a service or
product. It is generally for a limited time period and is designed to promote

consumer demand or increase awareness of products and services.[12] *Incentives* are gifts offered to attract customers. These can be coupons, reduced prices, two-for-one deals, and free merchandise or packets of useful materials.[13] Public libraries and school library media centers often provide free gifts to those who participate in parenting programs, summer reading activities, or reading achievement programs.

Publicity and Public Relations

Publicity in not-for-profit communication is designed to attract customers or users in positive ways to a product or service.[14] Publicity is widely used in libraries and can take the form of signs and slogans, website designs, public services announcements, and news releases. *Public relations*, closely related to publicity, is designed to produce free, positive mention of a product or service offered by an institution.[15] Libraries rely heavily on good public relations that have been systematically maintained over the years through the offering of quality services and programs. Public relationships can also be promoted through special events designed to enhance the image of the library. In Texas, the Texas Book Festival, inaugurated in 1995 by Laura Bush, First Lady of Texas, publicizes the work of Texas public libraries. Proceeds benefit public libraries in Texas. This was followed by a national book festival in 2001 that Bush organized as First Lady of the United States.

Message and Communication Designs

Design of messages was discussed at length in chapter 5. Essentially, it is how a desired idea is created and displayed so that it can be communicated effectively to an audience, thereby influencing the audience to learn about, believe in, and accept the values promoted in the message.[16] Communication is the transmission of a message to an audience, and *communication design* is the focused means of blending or mixing artistic design, psychological elements, knowledge of audience, and communication transmission elements into a unified message or messages designed to influence the behavior and attitudes of an audience.[17]

Atmospherics

Atmospherics are design factors closely associated with a physical place, such as a school library media center. They can influence how a service or product is received and accepted by an audience. Among other elements, atmospherics involve architecture, lighting, colors, furniture and its arrangement, and the use of art.[18] It can also involve staff dress and conduct. Librarian Mary Nichols suggests that place is important in marketing young adult collections, and the place selected for a community information center in the school library media center should also reflect these good atmospherics in design, comfort, and privacy.[19]

SUCCESS MEASUREMENTS AND THE AIDA MODEL

The communication strategy involving many of the above elements as used by a business is considered successful if members of the target audience understand and accept the product's message that the marketer is sending. The bottom line is *Are they buying or using the product or service that is being marketed?*

Toward this end, basic market strategy uses the AIDA model.[20] This model includes the following elements and seeks to obtain specific audience responses:

- A. Attention: The message is received and noticed.
- I. Interest: The message creates an interest in the product.
- D. Desire: The message creates a desire for the product.
- A. Action: The correct action is made to obtain the product.

MARKETING IN NONPROFIT SETTINGS

Because of the competition for resources, in recent decades nonprofit organizations, such as libraries, have had to become imaginative and aggressive in marketing their goods and services to their target audiences.

There are several major types of nonprofit marketing strategies widely used today. These include:[21]

- Person marketing;
- Place marketing;
- Idea marketing;
- Organization marketing.

Person marketing is designed to elicit a favorable response to a person associated with the organization and his or her ideas or contributions and skills. For example, the school library media center specialists can be marketed as people who have the knowledge and interest to provide helpful community information.

Place marketing within nonprofit marketing is designed to create a favorable attitude about a physical place. The school library media center can be marketed as a physical place that is convenient, comfortable, and nonjudgmental in terms of providing useful information, including community information.

Idea marketing is designed to promote a cause or issue important to a targeted audience. Perhaps the best example of idea marketing in the United

States is how the national government promotes an idea that it hopes will be accepted as a national policy. For example, years ago the American government established a policy of reducing the amount of smoking by the American people. Through information campaigns, the government sought to inform the public that smoking was not a good idea because it was harmful to one's health. Over the last thirty years, this message has been drummed into the American public's mind until now less than one-third of the adult population smokes. This campaign has been so successful that the claim is now made that the United States is a nonsmoking culture.

The last element of nonprofit marketing is *organization marketing*. This is marketing designed to attract members, donors, participants, or volunteers to aid a particular organization. The social, cultural, and educational values of an organization to community life are generally used to promote the organization to its target market. The American Red Cross and the American Cancer Society, as well as other organizations, are excellent examples of well-respected icons that are marketed as symbols of social good. Similarly, the school library media center can also create and market itself as an agency that helps ensure social good within the context of the school environment.

BASIC MARKETING TERMS AND SCHOOL LIBRARY MEDIA CENTER EXAMPLES

Before any kind of marketing can be done, the school library media center, like any corporate body, must understand its environment. In marketing, the area in which marketing is done is called the *marketing environment*. Good marketing is always based on knowledge of this environment. In technical terms, gaining knowledge of the intended market is called *scanning the environment*. Scanning the environment often involves tracing external changes that will affect markets, including the demand for goods and services. In business operations, these include issues such as the economy; political and legal considerations; the influence of social, institutional, and technological developments; and competitive factors. In school environments, these might include changes in curriculum, changes in the development and social needs of students, and demands from external sources such as government-mandated testing of students, colleges' and universities' admission requirements, and employers' expectations of student competencies.[22]

DETERMINANTS WITHIN THE MARKET ENVIRONMENT

One important factor found within the market environment is *demographic characteristics*. In marketing terms, demographic trends or characteristics help describe the social characteristics of the market environment. Good marketing strategies demand that marketers look at basic demographic data and characteristics of human populations. In general, these characteristics include, among others, age, birth rate, death rate, marital status, education, religion, ethnic background, immigration, and geographical distribution. When the demographic characteristics of a general market are known, then a strategy for marketing a product or service within that market can be better determined.[23] An understanding of the demographics of the schools—age, social and cultural backgrounds, economic circumstances, changes in neighborhood population patterns within its service boundaries—will greatly influence how a community information service can be developed and marketed.

Knowledge of demographics alone will not ensure that marketers have a solid grip on the intended market. School library media specialists must also understand the *cultural values* and *language* of their intended market. Cultural values are the principles or beliefs that members of a culture or society consider important and worthy of fostering.

Without question, culture and cultural values play a large role in determining how to design and market a community information program and service. Cultural values differ from country to country and even within a country, and cultural values can differ among social classes. Cultural values and behaviors can also vary from neighborhood to neighborhood. Good marketers of community information programs must make every effort to understand cultural variations and to take these into account when planning services and programs and in marketing those services. Community information services and its marketing in school environments must reflect the cultural values and behavior expectations of the school and the neighborhoods that it serves.[24]

Language plays an important role in defining culture and it too must be considered in marketing. Community information services must be ready to offer materials and translations of materials in languages other than English.[25]

Competition is also a part of not-for-profit marketing. In business, marketing must pay attention to its competition and how that competition will influence the acceptance of its products and services.[26] School library media centers as well as other types of libraries must be aware that they exist in a competitive environment and that there are several organizations that also can satisfy the needs and desires of their target markets. Books are available at bookstores; videotapes and CDs can be rented at video stores; all kinds of information, including community information, is now readily available over the Internet. How can school library media centers compete in such an information-rich environment? School library media centers can and will compete as all businesses compete. The school library media center can create good community information products and services that will meet the needs and desires of its target market. Through marketing, it can convince its target market that its community information program offers unique services that are convenient, reliable, and extremely useful and not available for the price elsewhere.

Another factor in marketing is the *technological environment* in which an organization lives. An ever-growing computer-literate society is aggressively demanding access to computer information technology, and most libraries continue to struggle to meet this market demand.[27] From a market point of view, community information in a school library media center must be technology-based. The Internet already offers community information, but is it disorganized. A competitive advantage held by the school library media center is that community information offered there can be more socially and culturally beneficial and educationally sound because it is subjected to rigorous selection and review processes that ensure it is suitable for the school market.

PERCEPTION: A BASIC ELEMENT IN A COMMUNITY INFORMATION MARKET CAMPAIGN

In chapter 5 we considered perception as an important element in presentation design.[28] *Perception* is also important in developing a marketing strategy. The following discussion relates to how it can be used in marketing.[29]

Marketers must take into account many social, cultural, and psychological factors in designing a market campaign. Perception is one such important psychological factor. An understanding of how a market audience perceives its social, educational, and cultural realities is fundamental to the successful marketing of community information services. Perception has practical meaning in how to design a market message. In other words, perception is basic to understanding how information is transmitted in society at all levels.

First, perception can be viewed as how people sense or become aware of their environment. Through perception, people come to an understanding of who they are as persons. Through perception, people come to understand their country, their city, their neighborhood, their home, and their family relationships. Perception is necessary in human life because it helps people to avoid chaos and to extract and organize information that comes to them from their immediate environment.

Psychologists, using data based on reliable research, tell us that people perceive in a very orderly fashion, although with limitations. People tend to perceive in large groups that relate to

- Relationships
- Events
- Groupings

- Words
- Objects
- People

Psychologists also tell us that, within these groupings, we can perceive only about seven items at one time. Beyond that, we as humans face information overload and then simply ignore much of the information presented. So when marketers design a market message they had best keep these principles in mind.

Another important aspect of perception is selectivity. Research again shows that we as humans select what we will perceive. This selection is based on

- Familiarity
- Past experiences
- Interests
- Needs

All these are important elements in marketing, including the marketing of community information services within a school context.

Familiarity. People tend to pay attention to, or at least feel comfortable with, what is familiar. Chances are that most users of school library media centers will be familiar with the center's major services, but the idea of community information may be an entirely new concept to them. If that is the case, a marketing strategy must develop and present an explanation of the concept that helps the audience become familiar with the idea and to accept it as a legitimate and needed service—a service that will benefit them individually.

Past experiences. The role of past experiences that people have had with libraries and school library media centers as convenient and pleasant places to find information and to receive service is important in marketing community information. Negative past experiences or even neutral experiences with libraries will need to be overcome with effective marketing strategies designed to modify these attitudes and to move the individual or audience toward more positive ways of accepting libraries and school library media centers. If past experiences with libraries have been positive, then a marketing strategy can be built on those experiences that enhance the perception that community information is a rich extension of library services.

Interests. Interests are favorable attitudes. The development of interest in humans is a sociopsychological phenomenon. As individuals, we develop our interests based on these two basic elements: the social environment in which we live and our individual psychological needs, which give direction and help form our interests. Some have said that of these two, the social element has more influence.

It is society and our culture that influence the formation of our interests. For example, interests are often formed and cultivated because they promote an acceptable social appearance and status. On the other hand, interests are also introspective. That is, they often satisfy our individual need for psychological support. Whatever the cause, interests are serious and introspective. A marketing strategy for community information must certainly understand and draw upon the interests of the intended market.

Needs. All marketing strategies must focus on needs. Often a commercial marketing strategy is to create a need for the product or service where one does not exist. In the case of a community information program, the assumption can be made that members of this target group need community information for many good reasons. In this way community information

- Supports information literacy;
- Contributes to the curriculum and program of study;
- Promotes a broad understanding of modern culture and society;
- Provides for personal assistance;
- Helps prepare students for life.

Based on these principles, marketers need to be aware that perception principles indicate that people will attend to only selected messages, and this is based to a large part on needs, past experiences, and conditions. Perception will also influence the way a message is interpreted and what is remembered from the message based on existing beliefs and values.[30] With this understanding of perception, a marketing strategy can then be developed that reminds the target audience that a center's community information program and services can meet many of their needs, while reinforcing their positive values and beliefs.

STRATEGIES FOR SOCIAL MARKETING

As mentioned earlier, social marketing is based on the principles of marketing, and many of these strategies have proved effective in a number of well-known social marketing campaigns. Researchers Kotler, Roberto, and Lee have identified the following as among some of the most interesting and well-conceived social marketing campaigns:[31]

- The National High Blood Pressure Education Program (National Institute of Health, U.S. Government program)
  - Message: "Protect Your Health! Prevent High Blood Pressure"
- Salmon Recovery Program (City of Seattle and Seattle Public Utilities)
  - Messages: "Be a Salmon Friendly Gardener" and "How to Be a Salmon Friendly Gardener"
- Florida Cares for Women Program (Florida Health Department [breast cancer prevention])
  - Message: "A Special Gift for Women 50 and Over. Once a Year Peace of Mind. Gentle, Affordable, Breast & Cervical Cancer Screenings."

From a strategy perspective, all these campaigns have the following characteristics in common; they have:[32]

- Analyzed the social market environment;
- Selected the target audience;
- Determined the background and situation that promote the need for the social message within the audience and analyzed support and cooperation available for the campaign;
- Formulated goals and objectives;
- Profiled the target audience and the competition that will challenge the campaign within the audience;
- Determined specific strategies, including
  - Product development (e.g., services, information that promote positive behaviors)
  - Pricing (cost to audience in adopting the positive behaviors)
  - Place (deciding where the positive action can take place)
  - Promotion (deciding on ways and means of disseminating information and of increasing awareness and understanding of the social message using):
    - ✔ Fact sheets, pamphlets, brochures, Internet;
    - ✔ Guidelines for professionals with information about how to promote the desired behaviors;
    - ✔ Websites with specific information;
    - ✔ Contact information (e.g., toll-free numbers, recorded information);
    - ✔ Special materials for subgroups within the audience;
    - ✔ Special materials attuned to language and cultural needs;
    - ✔ Mass media dissemination (news releases, print advertisement, radio, television, and posters);
    - ✔ Special events and programs.
- Evaluated ways and means of monitoring and determining positive behavior changes within the target market;
- Established a budget and secured funding sources.

LIBRARIES AND SOCIAL MARKETING

Public relationship and good public images have always been important to the library community, and in recent years, marketing has taken its place alongside the need to promote libraries. Based on the literature of marketing within library and information studies, social marketing as a concept appears to be relatively new to the field.

Kathryn Leide, a spokesperson for ALA Graphics, wrote this about the need to promote the library in the community, and her remarks reinforce many of the elements of social marketing:[33]

We, as a profession, must promote libraries more than we have ever before. We must take the time and energy and resources to let communities know that we are a vital link to information and crucial if we are to have equality of access.

She goes on to say that library posters need to leave library walls and go out into the community and that ALA helps this effort through its production of public awareness materials and by providing digital and license image products that will allow libraries to produce their own individualized posters and other materials suitable for promoting their services and products within their own communities.[34]

A recent example of this effort includes materials produced for Teen Read Week of 2003 that provide ALA-endorsed promotions for schools and libraries. Another recently produced item is the Whoopi Goldberg–narrated film "America's Libraries Change Lives." In 1993, the Association of School Libraries also produced Kaleidoscope: New Visions for School Library Media Program (Follett Software Co.), intended to influence school administrators, teachers, parents, school staff members, and others about the importance of school library media centers using social marketing principles. In fact, ALA and its divisions over the years have produced numerous social marketing materials. These include news releases and radio and television public service announcements—all intended to influence positive attitudes and behaviors regarding libraries in society.[35]

Social marketing offers an avenue that not only explains the goals and mission of the school library media center and its community information program but also, if used correctly, has the potential to influence users' attitudes and behaviors in positive ways about the service and roles offered by school library media centers and libraries in general in all democratic societies. Social marketing can also play a part in the overall process of socializing students to live better and more productive lives through the better use of all types of information.

In addition to promotional strategies, merchandizing practices and sign systems can also be used alongside the usual advertising and public relations efforts (e.g., media uses, promotional message and strategies, and special presentations).

MERCHANDISING, DISPLAY, AND SIGN SYSTEMS

Merchandising and the display of merchandise are important elements in the success of any community information service. Many of the elements of merchandising have already been discussed in this and previous chapters, including market elements, design factors, and psychological influences. Displays are essential to good community information merchandising. In planning quarters for community information, careful consideration should be given to literature racks where giveaway or quick reference materials can be easily accessible. Commercially available modes include tabletop, free-standing, and wall-mounted designs, and slatwall displays units. Combined display and divider systems are also useful for community information. This type of combination can be used for posting community announcements and information and for helping to direct and control traffic patterns.

As mentioned previously, bulletin boards are hallmarks of community information. Bulletin boards can be mounted on a wall or they can be mobile units. A slatwall and bulletin board make a viable combination for community information.[36] Other items to consider in promoting community information include small display easels for exhibiting reinforced posters and other forms of community information.

Sign systems are a necessary part of the community information center program. Signs call attention to services and direct people to important information units. Sign systems also help form positive user behaviors and reinforce useful decision-making skills of users by offering prompts for action.

A good system must first provide orientation for the user to the environment, offering a sense of place (e.g., "You Are Here"). In doing this, the sign system will offer the user a mental map of place, helping the user better understand the environment (e.g., map of school library media center, showing the community information center).

Sign systems will also assist the user in making individual adjustments and in deciding on actions to take within the environment. (See Figure 7.1.)

An understanding of the perceptional base (e.g., familiarity, past experiences, need, interests, etc.) of the user is important because this understanding will help develop sign systems that help the user focus and reduce anxiety and confusion. Sign systems based on perceptional understanding can intro-

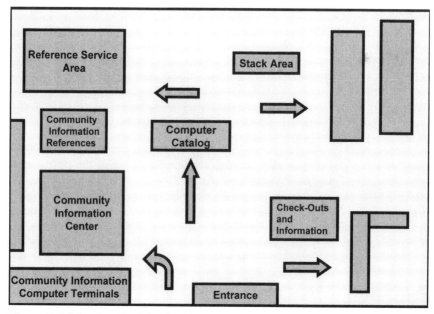

Figure 7.1 Mapping the School Library Media Center for Community Information

duce familiar behavior clues, such as arrows, logos, colors, and strong words such as "Obtain Community Information Here." Strongly worded statements offer clear orientation cues and help form positive behavior patterns.

Both novelty of sign design and simplicity are necessary integrants of sign systems. Novelty will attract attention, but all sign systems must be simple and offer clearly stated information. Sign systems must not be overloaded with too much information. The overuse of signs must likewise be avoided. As stated, signs are provided to help with orientation and to encourage the development of positive behavior—not to offer complete information on how to proceed within a library's environment or to provide detailed information on polices of operation. More detailed information about such management concerns can be provided through other means, such as booklets, leaflets, and other forms of printed materials. Finally, sign systems must be professionally created, avoiding a sense of amateurism in art work and conceptual design.[37]

CONCLUSION

All marketing programs must have a clearly articulated and understood strategy. Based on a clear understanding of the principles of marketing, especially social marketing, school library media center programs can do much in promoting the use and acceptance of community information. As field research conducted for this book reveals (chapter 6), this concept is new to many school library media specialists, and many different definitions or concepts about it exist in the school library media center professional community. This level of unfamiliarity and uncertainty calls for marketing strategies both at the local school level and at the broader professional level that will explain the usefulness of community information to the individual as well as to the school. Schools as a social institution are charged with the mission of responding to the varied information needs of society, and community information services and programs within the school library media center can greatly enhance that mission.

NOTES

1. Gilbert A. Churchill and J. Paul Peter, *Marketing: Creating Value for Customers* (Burr Ridge, Ill.: Austin Press, 1995), 7.
2. Ibid.
3. Ibid., 123.
4. Ibid., 16, 119–150, 307.
5. Ibid., 16–18.
6. Mary Ann Nichols, *Merchandising Library Materials to Young Adults* (Greenwood Village, Colo.: Libraries Unlimited, 2002), 3.
7. Philip Kotler and others, *Social Marketing: Improving the Quality of Life*, 2nd ed. (Thousand Oaks, Calif.: Sage, 2002), 217.

8. Nedra Kline Weinreich, "What Is Social Marketing?" Weinreich Communications, webmaster@social-marking.com, available at http://www.social-marketing.com/Whatis.html.

9. Churchill and Peter, 18, 514, 575–76, 681, 682.

10. Ibid., 675.

11. Ibid., 678.

12. Ibid., 682.

13. Kotler and others, 226–28.

14. Churchill and Peter, 682.

15. Kotler and others, 292.

16. Ibid., 42.

17. Churchill and Peter, 676.

18. Ibid., 674; Nichols, 3–4.

19. Nichols.

20. Churchill and Peter, 541, 574.

21. Ibid., 19.

22. Ibid., 33.

23. Ibid., 46.

24. Ibid., 48–50.

25. Ibid., 50–51.

26. Ibid., 54–59.

27. Ibid., 52–54.

28. Malcolm Fleming and W. Howard Levie, *Instructional Message Design: Principles from the Behavioral Sciences* (Englewood Cliffs, N.J.: Educational Technology Publications, 1978), 3–95.

29. Churchill and Peter, 240–42.

30. Ibid., 242.

31. Kotler and others, 30–31, 36–37, 42, 88.

32. Ibid., 30–33, 34, 39.

33. *ALA Graphics, 2003 Summer Catalog* (Chicago: American Library Association, 2003), 1.

34. Ibid.

35. American Library Association Archives. Record Group: Public Relations Office. Publications, Sound Recordings, 1960–1992, 1996. Description. Record Group: American Association of School Librarians, Executive Secretary, 1991–1992. Record Serial No. 20/2/6. Description of File notes. Available at www.library/uiuc.edu/ahx/ala/ccard/ALAControlCard.asp?RG=12&SG=3&SG=3&RS=13 and www.library.uiuc.edu/ahx/ala/ccard/ALAControlCard.asp?RG=20&SG=2&RS=6.

36. Nichols, 74–89.

37. Dorothy Pollet and Peter C. Haskell, *Sign Systems for Libraries: Solving the Wayfinding Problem* (New York: R. R. Bowker, 1979), 4–14.

CHAPTER 8

Challenges for the Future

INTRODUCTION

The world at the beginning of the twenty-first century faces many challenges. It appears to be a world in which basic values of human life are being tested to a degree never before encountered, mainly because of the advances in technology and human interaction. On the one hand, the world faces terrorism and the destruction of many social orders and cultural values; on the other hand, we face the demands of increasing globalization and multiculturalism.

COMMUNITY AND SOCIETY IN A GLOBAL CONTEXT

Community information at the local level can and must play a role in this period of cultural, political, and social transformation. Although local community information serves the localized and immediate needs of students in their neighborhoods and lives, it is the building block of globalization and multiculturalism. It introduces students to the real world and to information that reflects the dynamics of the world and how people cope with the demands placed on them by changing societies. (See Figure 8.1).

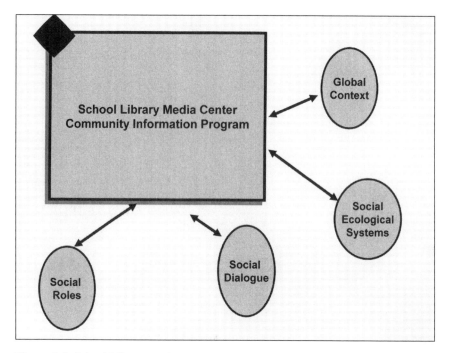

Figure 8.1 School Library Media Center Community Information in a Global Context

COMMUNITY INFORMATION AND SOCIAL ROLES

Community information also can help students learn about roles in society and the options they have for defining their own unique roles as they move into adulthood. It likewise helps them consider, through the types of information available to them in their communities, how people and institutions interact and support each other.

SOCIAL ECOLOGICAL SYSTEMS AND COMMUNITY INFORMATION

All people exist in an ecological system. Over time, human ecological systems develop and require complex patterns of relationships that are affected by multiple levels of environmental conditions. These include the immediate family and school as well as broader cultural values, programs, and services that support these values. Community information as a part of information literacy has the potential for helping students think actively about their role in their particular ecological system.

In seeking to find their own social structures, students, in essence, create their own social realities through dialogue and other forms of interactions.

In this way, they make sense of the life that they experience. We know that students as well as all of us are constantly involved in social dialogues of many types as we seek to understand our place in our society and world. Dialogue with diverse courses of information is necessary to ensure an adequate sense of self and society.

COMMUNITY INFORMATION AND SOCIAL DIALOGUE

Students, like adults, acquire their ways of thinking and behaving that generally reinforce their community's values through cooperative dialogues with knowledgeable and informed members of the community. Unfortunately, not all students form dialogues with constructive elements in their communities. Community information, organized and presented in attractive and age-appropriate ways, can compensate in many ways for faulty dialogues and communications that are available to students in some communities.

COMMUNITY INFORMATION: IMPORTANT FOR THE SCHOOL LIBRARY MEDIA CENTER

School library media centers have a well-defined role to play in modern education. It is one of the important parts of all progressive educational systems. Over the years, the school library media center's functional and theoretical roles have been well developed and defined. Because of this systematic historical development, a well-understood paradigm explaining the function of the school library media center is in place and is well disseminated through formal educational programs, publications, conferences, and other means of paradigm development. It is this function and role in terms of information provision and delivery that ensures that the school library media center will play an ever-increasing role in making community information available to students. Students will benefit from this in their daily lives as they move into the global world of the twenty-first century.

Examples of a Local School Subject Headings Authority List

Appropriate subject descriptors can add greatly to the effectiveness of a local school community information system. The following is a list of subject descriptors used in previous years to access local school topics in the vertical file of the University of North Texas, Denton, Texas (formerly North Texas State University). In this file, all descriptors were preceded by the name of the institution, followed by a dash:

(Example: **NTSU—Alumni**). This list has been adjusted to reflect how such a list can be used in elementary and secondary schools: (Example: **Johnson High School—Assemblies**).

A

Alumni
Assemblies
Athletics (Subdivide A–Z). *See also* Departments—Health, physical education and recreation

- Baseball
- Boxing
- Fencing

Examples of Local School Headings Authority List. Published with permission of the School of Library and Information Science, University of North Texas.

- Football
- Golf
- Gymnastics
- Swimming
- Tennis
- Track and field
- Trapshooting
- Volleyball
- Weight lifting

B

Bands and orchestras. *Refer from* (xx) Organizations and activities: Departments—Music
Budget
Buildings (Subdivide A–Z)

C

Cafeteria
Campus
Charities
Counseling. *Refer from* (x) Vocational guidance

D

Debates
Departments. *See also*

- Agriculture
- Art
- Biology
- Business education
- Chemistry
- Economics and sociology
- English
- Foreign languages
- Geography
- Government
- Health, physical education and recreation. *Refer from* (xx) Athletics
- History
- Home economics
- Industrial arts
- Journalism
- Mathematics

- Music
- Physics
- Psychology
- Speech and drama

Diplomas
Directories

E–F

Enrollment
Exhibits
Faculty and staff (Subdivide A–Z). *See also* Principals
Faculty and staff—Collective
Fine arts. *See also* Programs. *Refer from* (xx) Departments

G–H

Gifts and memorials. *Refer from* (x) Memorials
Graduation

- Annual
- Summer
- Winter

Herbarium
History
Homecoming

I–M

Interscholastic league
Library. *See* Library Media Center
Library Media Center
Mascot
Memorials. *See* Gifts and memorials
Music festivals. *See* Fine arts; Programs

N–P

News releases and services
Organizations (Subdivide A–Z)
Principals (Subdivide A–Z)
Programs. *Refer from* (xx) Departments
Publications

R–S

Radio and television broadcasting
Scholarships and loan funds (Subdivide A–Z)
Social sciences, Department of. *See* Departments (Subdivide A–Z)
Songs
Student self-government

T

Television
Traditions
Trophies

W–Z

Vocational guidance. *See* Counseling
Wars (Subdivide A–Z)

Starter List of Local City and Area File Subject Headings

The list of suggested subject headings provides a means of beginning or expanding an existing file of local community information. These headings reflect the general concept of attempting to anticipate what students will need as they seek information within the community. No attempt has been made to be exhaustive in approach. The school media library specialist will need to consult other sources for other subject headings as needed. The local phonebook and Yellow Pages will be extremely helpful in finding subject headings unique to the local situation.

In most cases, these subject headings should reflect the local situations, and this is generally done by placing the name of the local geographic designator in front of the subject heading (e.g., **Chicago—Adoption and foster home care**). Several appropriate but related local geographic designators may also be used. For example: **Austin** (for city); **Travis County** (for county); **Austin-Travis County** (for combined administrative area, and Austin Metropolitan Area for a large service area).

Local proper names may also be added directly, that is, without using the subject terms after the main geographic designator (e.g., **Austin—Hogg Foundation**). Proper names of locally important geographic features, among others, also may be added directly as needed. Example: **Austin—Balcones Fault Line** (for a well-known geological feature).

Avoid as much as possible the creation of multi-levels of subject subheadings. This can be done by using general headings. For example, instead of having individual files for biographies, place information about individuals in a general biography file, for example, **Austin—Biography** (A–Z). Information about professional groups can be handled in two ways: **Occupations and careers** (A–Z) or by using subject headings for specific occupations and careers (e.g., **Dentistry**).

Access to local community information can also be served by entering the proper name first rather than the geographic designator heading. This can help if the file becomes excessively large. This alternative approach calls for local proper names to be entered first in the subject heading, followed by a geographic designator. For example, the subject heading for Planned Parenthood of Austin can be established as **Planned Parenthood of Austin (Austin, Texas)** and filed alphabetically in the local history file. This approach is possible even when the general practice is to establish headings according to geographic designators. For example, a file might look something like this:

AIDS Service of Austin Inc. (Austin, Texas)
American Civil Liberties Union (Austin, Texas)
Austin—Adoption and foster home care
Austin—Air and air quality programs and services
Austin Symphonic Band (Austin, Texas)

In order to simplify this list, *see also* references have not been provided. *Use* reference points found in the guide may be adapted as *see* references and added to the file if *see* references are needed. Additional subject headings may be adapted from *The Vertical File Index* (H. W. Wilson), *Sears List of Subject Headings*, online catalogs; and various youth-oriented sites available on the World Wide Web.

A

Accountants (collective)
    For individuals use Biography
ADA
    Use Americans with Disabilities Act
Adoption and foster home care
African Americans (collective)
    For individual African American use Biography
    Note: Appropriate subheadings for this and all ethnic groups may be added. Consult a recent edition of *Sears List of Subject Headings* and other recognized subject authority files for suggested subheadings, such as Authors, Folklore, Songs and Music, etc.
Aged
    Use Senior citizens

Agriculture
AIDS and HIV services (A–Z)
AIDS information
   Use AIDS and HIV services
Air and air quality programs (A–Z)
Airports (A–Z)
Americans with Disabilities Act
Animals and animal welfare
   Names of organizations, institutions may be added (e.g., Austin Area—
   Wildlife Rescue)
Apartments
   Names of apartments may be added directly (e.g., Austin—Apartments,
   Live Oaks Apartments)
Archaeology
Architects (collective)
   For individuals use Biography
Architecture
Archives (A–Z)
Archivists (collective)
   For individual archivists use Biography
Art
Art in public places
   Use Art, Public
Art—Painting
Art, Public
Artists (A–Z) (collective)
   For individual artists use Biography
Artists' guilds (A–Z)
Arts and crafts
   Use Crafts

Associations and organizations (A–Z)
   Names of associations and organizations may be added directly (e.g.,
   Austin—Texas Civil Liberties Union)
Authors (collective)
   For individual authors use Biography

B

Babysitting
Biography (A–Z)
Bikes and biking
Birth control programs and services (A–Z)

Names of programs and services may be added directly (e.g., Austin—
Planned Parenthood of Austin).

Blacks
    Use African Americans
Blind
Boats and boating
Body image
Book clubs
    Use Reading and book clubs
Books and reading
Bridges (A–Z)
Businesses (A–Z)
Buses and bus routes
    Names of bus and bus families may be added directly (e.g., Austin—
    Capitol Metro bus facilities)
Broadcasting

C

Cable television (A–Z)
Calendars and schedules
Canada postal code
    Use Postal Code, Canada
Careers
    Use Occupations and careers
Cartoons, Political
    Use Political cartoons
Catholic Churches (Roman)
    Use Churches (A–Z)
Cellular phones
Cemeteries (A–Z)
Censorship and obscenity
Charities (A–Z)
Charters, City and county (A–Z)
Charters, Organizations and institutions (A–Z)
Chemical industry
    Use Industries
Child abuse
Child care
Child health services (A–Z)
Children's programs and services (A–Z)
Christmas
    Use Holidays
Churches (A–Z)
    Names of churches may be added directly (e.g., Austin—Congress Avenue
    Baptist Church)

City council
    Use City government
City government (A–Z)
City offices (A–Z)
City planning
Climate
Community access television broadcasting (A–Z)
Companies—History (A–Z)
Classes and instructions (A–Z)
Coin collectors (collective)
    For individual coin collectors use Biography (A–Z)
Coin collecting
    Use Hobbies
College and Universities (A–Z)
Community kitchens
    Names of community meal services may be added directly (e.g., Austin—
    Meals on Wheels and More).
Cookery (A–Z)
    Name of cookery and cooking styles may be added directly (e.g., Austin—
    Cookery—Tex Mex).
County government (A–Z)
County—Offices (A–Z)
    Names of county offices may be added directly (e.g., Travis County—
    County Offices—District Clerk)
Courts and court jurisdictions (A–Z)
    Names of courts and jurisdictions may be added directly (e.g., Austin—
    Municipal Court no. 1)
Clubs and organizations (A–Z)
    Names of organizations may be added directly (e.g., Travis County—
    Clubs and organizations—4-H Clubs).
Computers
Counseling and guidance services (A–Z)
Crafts (A–Z)
Crime
Crime victims
    Use Victims of crimes, programs and services
Crisis centers, programs and service (A–Z)

D

Dating, Teen
    Use Teen dating
Death and dying programs (A–Z)
    Name of programs and services may be added directly (e.g., Austin—
    Circle of Life Hospice)

Delivery programs and services
    Use Postal and delivery services and programs
Dentists (collective)
    For individual dentists use Biography
Dentistry
Disabled—Ordinances
    Use Ordinances and codes
Disabled persons (collective)
Disabled services and programs
Disaster preparation and help
Disasters (A–Z)
Distance learning and distance learning programs (A–Z)
    Name of distance learning programs may be added directly (e.g., Austin—
    University of Texas at Austin, College of Engineering, Center for Life-
    long Engineering Education)
Drug and alcohol abuse programs and services (A–Z)

E

Eating disorders
Economic assistance, Domestic
Education (A–Z)
Education, Elementary
Education, Higher
Education, Secondary
Election information and guides
Elections (A–Z)
Emergency medical services
Employment
    Use Jobs and job information
Energy conservation and programs
Engineers (collective)
    For individuals use Biography
Environmental groups
    Use Associations and organizations
Environmental services and programs (A–Z)
Episcopal churches
    Use Churches
Events (A–Z)
    Use Calendars
Exercise
Exhibitions and exhibition centers (A–Z)
    Names of exhibitions and exhibition centers may be added directly (e.g.,

Austin—Palmer Auditorium; Travis County—Travis County Exhibition Hall; Austin—Olympic Ice Skating Exhibitions [date]).

Express highways (A–Z)
 Names of highways may be added directly (e.g., Austin—Republic of Texas Highway)

Eye care and surgery centers
 Use Hospitals

F

Fairs and festivals (A–Z)
Families and family life (A–Z)
Fire department and stations (A–Z)
Fish and fishing
Flood control
Folk and urban lore
Food stamp programs
 Specific names of programs may be added directly (e.g., Austin Metropolitan Area—Lone Star Food Stamp Program)
Foster care
 Use Adoption and foster care

G

Garbage and garbage collection services
Genealogy (A–Z)
 Names of families may be added directly (e.g., Austin—Genealogy—Blalock Family)
Geology and geological features (A–Z)
 Names of individual geological features may be added directly (e.g., Austin—Balcones Fault Line)
Government documents
 Use Government publications
Government publications
Groundwater
 Use Water, Underground

H

Halloween
 Use Holidays
Health and health services (A–Z)
Highways, Express (A–Z)

Hiking and hiking trails (A–Z)
Historians (collective)
  For individual historians use Biography
Historic areas (A–Z)
  Names of well-known historic areas may be added directly (e.g., Travis
  County—Plum Creek, Battle of)
Historic homes and buildings (A–Z)
  Name of historic homes and building may be added directly (e.g., Austin—
  French Legation).
Historic landmarks (A–Z)
  Name of official historic landmarks, other than historic homes or build-
  ings, may be added directly (e.g., Austin—"Treaty Oaks Site").
Historic preservation services and programs (A–Z)
History (A–Z)
  (Note: This heading must always be proceeded by a geographic designator
  (e.g., Austin— History).
Hobbies (A–Z)
Hospitals (A–Z)
Hotels and motels (A–Z)
Hotlines
  Use Crisis centers, programs and services

I

Incentive and awards programs (A–Z)
Indians of North America
  Use Native Americans
Industry (A–Z)
Information and referral services and programs (A–Z)
Insurance (A–Z)
Interior decorators (collective)
  For individual interior decorators use Biography

J

Jails and jail programs (A–Z)
  Names of jails and jail programs may be added directly (e.g., Austin—State
  Jail Facility)
Jobs and job information (A–Z)
  See also Work and work places
Judges (collective)
  (Note: Use Courts and court jurisdictions for jurisdictional affairs. Use
  Biography for information about individuals.)

Justices of the Peace (collective)
    For individual justices of the peace use Biography
Justices of the peace offices (A–Z)
    Use Courts and court jurisdictions
Juvenile delinquency services and programs
    Name of juvenile delinquent services and programs may be added directly
    (e.g., Travis County—Juvenile Probations; Travis County—Gardner Betts
    Juvenile Justice Center)

K

Kennels
    Use Animals and animal welfare
Kites and gliders
    Use Hobbies
Kung-Fu instruction
    Use Classes and instruction

L

Landscape architects (collective)
    For individuals use Biography
Landscaping and landscaped areas (A–Z)
    Names of landscaped areas may be added directly (e.g., Austin—Botani-
    cal Garden)
Leadership programs and services (A–Z)
Libraries (A–Z)
    Names of libraries may be added directly (e.g., Austin—Texas State Li-
    brary and Archives)
Literacy and literacy programs (A–Z)
    Names of literacy and literacy programs may be added directly (e.g., Aus-
    tin—Austin Reads)
Litter and littering
Law enforcement (A–Z)
    Names of law enforcement agencies may be added directly (e.g., Austin—
    Park Police)
Legal services and programs (A–Z)
    Names of legal services and programs may be added directly (e.g., Travis
    County— Juvenile Public Defender)
Licenses and permits (A–Z)
    Name of licenses and permits may be added directly (e.g., Austin—Texas
    Drivers License Offices)

M

Magazines
    Use Newspapers and magazines
Mail services and programs
    Use Postal and delivery services and programs
Malls, shopping
    Use Shopping centers
Maps
    Use (Location)—Maps (e.g., Travis County—Maps)
    Use (Location) Street maps (e.g., Austin—Street maps)
Martial arts (A–Z)
    Use Sports
Medical care (A–Z)
Medical care, Emergency
    Use Emergency medical services
Military programs and services (A–Z)
    Names of military programs and services may be added directly (e.g., Austin—Marine Corps).
Mosques (A–Z)
    Names of mosques may be added directly (e.g., Austin—Islamic Ahlul Bayt Association of the).
Museums (A–Z)
    Names of associations, organizations, institutions, etc., may be added directly (e.g., Austin—Austin Children's Museum)
Music
Musicians (collective)
    For individual musicians use Biographies

N

National Register of Historic Places (A–Z)
Native Americans (collective)
    For individual Native Americans use Biography
    For other subheadings refer to examples listed under African Americans
Neighborhoods and neighborhood programs (A–Z)
    Names of neighborhoods and neighborhood associations may be added directly (e.g., Austin—Travis Park Neighborhood Association)
Newspapers and magazines (A–Z)
    Names of newspapers and magazines published in the geographic area or associated with the geographic area may be added directly (e.g., Austin—*Austin Statesman American*)
Nutrition

O

Organizations
  Use Associations and organizations

P

Parent-Teacher Association (A–Z)
Parks (A–Z)
Pay television
  Use Cable television
Performing arts and performing arts programs (A–Z)
  Names of performing arts organizations and programs may be added directly (e.g., Austin—Austin Lyric Opera)
Permits
  Use Licenses and permits
Photographers (collective)
  For individual photographers use Biographies
Photography
Planning and planning programs (A–Z)
Police (A–Z)
Political cartoons
Political parties
  Names of individual political parties may be added directly (e.g., Travis County—Democratic Party; Travis County—Republican Party)
Politics and government
Pollution
  Use Air and air quality programs
Population characteristics
Population statistics
  Use Population characteristics
Ports, River and sea (A–Z)
Post Code, United Kingdom
  May be subdivided geographically, e.g., Post Code, United Kingdom—London)
Postal and delivery programs and services (A–Z)
  Name of programs and services may be added directly (e.g., Austin—U.S. Post Offices and Services; Austin—United Parcel Service [UPS]).
Postal Code, Canada
  May subdivide geographically, e.g., Postal Code, Canada—Toronto)
Postal codes
  Names of postal codes of individual countries may be added directly using the official names of the codes (e.g., Post Code, United Kingdom, Postal Code, Canada; Zip Code, United States)

Postal delivery code
  Use Postal codes
Pregnancy and pregnancy programs (A–Z)
  Names of pregnancy programs may be added directly (e.g., Austin Metro-
  politan Area— Women's Infant's and Children's Program [WIC])
Preventive health services for children
  Use Health and health services
Private schools (A–Z)
  Use Schools, Private
Probation services and programs (A–Z)
  Name of probation services and programs may be added directly (e.g.,
  Travis County—Juvenile Home and Court)
Public school systems and districts
  Use Schools, Public school systems and districts
Public spaces
  Names of widely recognized public spaces may be added directly (e.g.,
  Austin—"Town Lake")

Q–R

Quality of life
  Use Standards of living
Quarries and quarrying
Radio
  Use Radio and television
Railroads (A–Z)
Railroads—History (A–Z)
Rape and rape prevention programs (A–Z)
Reading clubs
  Use Books and reading clubs
Recreation and recreation programs and services (A–Z)
  Name of programs and services may be added directly (e.g., Austin—
  South Austin Little League)
Recycling (Waste, etc.)
  Use Garbage and garbage programs
Rehabilitation centers (A–Z)
  Name of rehabilitation centers may be added directly (e.g., Austin—Doris
  Miller Recreation Center)
Religious organizations (A–Z)
  Names of religious organizations may be added directly (e.g., Austin
  Metropolitan Area—Austin Area Interreligious Ministries)
Relocation (Housing)
Restaurants (A–Z)

Reunions (A–Z)
Reunions, School (A–Z)

S

Sales tax
Schools, Private (A–Z)
    Names of private schools may be added as directly (e.g., Austin—Austin
    Learning Academy)
Schools, Public school systems and districts (A–Z)
    Names of public school systems and districts may be added directly (e.g.,
    Austin—Austin Independent School District)
Schools, Secondary and elementary (A–Z)
    (Note: Includes middle schools)
Self-defense (A–Z)
Self-help
    Use Counseling and guidance services
Senior citizens
    (Note: Includes information about senior citizens such as social and cul-
    tural groups)
Senior citizens programs and services (A–Z)
    Names of programs and services may be added directly (e.g., Austin—
    Family Eldercare)
Sex crimes, Victims of
    Use Victims of crimes, programs and services
Sexual harassment
Sexuality, Youth
Sexually transmitted diseases programs and services (A–Z)
    Name of programs and services may be added directly (e.g., Austin—AIDS
    Services of Austin, Inc.)
Shopping centers (A–Z)
    Names of shopping centers may be added directly (e.g., Austin—Baton
    Creek Square Mall).
Social service agencies and programs and services (A–Z)
    Names of programs and services may be added directly (e.g., Austin—
    Meals on Wheels And More).
Social welfare programs and services
    Use Social service agencies and programs and services
Social workers (collective)
    For individual social workers use Biography
Soil and soil improvement programs (A–Z)
Standards of living

STD
  Use Sexually transmitted diseases services and programs
Stone quarries
  Use Quarries and quarrying
Stores, Retail (A–Z)
  Names of well-known retails stores may be added directly (e.g., Austin—
  Sears Roebuck and Company)
Storytelling and storytelling programs (A–Z)
Street maps
  Use Maps
Street planning
Street persons, Programs and services for (A–Z)
Street safety programs and services (A–Z)
Streets (A–Z)
  Names of well-known streets may be added directly (e.g., Austin—
  Streets—Congress Avenue)
Suffrage movements
Suicide and suicide prevention programs (A–Z)
Synagogues (A–Z)
  Name of synagogues may be added directly (e.g., Austin—Beth Chaim
  Messianic Congregation (UMJC)

T

Taxation
Teachers and school employees (collective)
  For individual teachers and school employees use Biography
Teenage dating
Teenage driving
Teenage parents, Programs and services for (A–Z)
  Names of programs and services may be added directly (e.g., Austin—
  Marywood Children & Family Services)
Teenage runaways
Teenage violence
Telecommunications and telecommunications programs (A–Z)
Telecourses
  Use Distant learning and distant learning programs (A–Z)
Television
  Use Radio and television
Temples (A–Z)
  Names of temples may be added directly (e.g., Austin—Masonic Temple)
Tests, Placement
  Use Pupil progression plan

Theaters, Buildings
  Use Buildings
Theater programs (A–Z)
  Names of theater program may be added directly (e.g., Austin Metro-
  politan Area— Lockhart Community Theater, Lockhart, Texas)
Tobacco
Tours and Tourist Information programs and services (A–Z)
  Names of tours and tourist information programs and services may be
  added directly (e.g., Austin—Walking Tours; Austin—Austin Convention
  and Visitors Bureau)
Trade unions (A–Z)
  Names of trade unions may be added directly, (e.g., Austin—Texas Fed-
  eration of Teachers)
Transportation (A–Z)
  Names of transportation offices, bureaus, and facilities may be added di-
  rectly (e.g., Austin—Capitol Metro (bus facilities); Austin—Aviation, City
  Department of)

U

Unions
  Use Trade unions
United Kingdom, Post Code
  Use Post Code, United Kingdom
U.S. Zip Code
  Use Zip Code, United States

V–W

Victims of crimes, programs and services (A–Z)
  Names of programs may be added directly (e.g., Austin—Victims of
  Crime, Police Dept.)
Vocational education
  Names of organizations and vocational schools, etc., may be added di-
  rectly (e.g., Austin—Southern Careers Institute)
Volunteer programs and services (A–Z)
Voting and voting rights
Water and water programs and services (A–Z)
  Names of water programs and services may be added directly (Austin Met-
  ropolitan Area— Lower Colorado River Authority)
Water, Underground
  Names of underground water reservoirs may be added directly (e.g.,
  Austin Metropolitan Area—Edwards Underground Aquifer)

Weather
    Use Climate
Wild flowers
    Name of organization and institutions promoting wildflowers may be
    added directly (e.g., Austin—Lady Bird Johnson Wildflower Center)
Women (collective)
    For individual women use Biography
Women—History
Work and work places
    Names of work programs and centers may be added directly (e.g., Austin—
    HHSC Job Center). Also names of historically important workers and work
    places may be added (e.g., Austin—Telephone workers)

X–Y–Z

Youth and youth programs (A–Z)
    Names of youth programs may be added directly (Austin Metropolitan
    Area—Camp Fire Boys & Girls, Capital Area Council).
Zip Code, United States
    May be subdivided geographically (e.g., Zip Code, United States—Austin,
    Texas)
Zoning and zoning codes
Zoos and zoological gardens (A–Z)
    Names of zoos and zoological gardens may be added directly (e.g.,
    Austin—Austin Zoo; Austin—Snake Farm)

Focus Group and Field Survey Materials

SECTION 1. COMMUNITY INFORMATION IN SCHOOL LIBRARIES TRANSCRIPT OF QUESTIONS AND FOCUS GROUP RESPONSES

Conducted March 26, 2003

1. Which of the following definitions of community are you most comfortable with?

    A. Community is defined by geographic boundaries
    B. Community is more a state of mind, an image

RESPONSES:

- Cultural origins, different languages representing 40 countries
- Extended families
- Neighborhood
- School community (teachers/parents)
- Different backgrounds
- Neighborhood around school (*see illustration*)
- Different sections of town (e.g., business partnerships)
- "Community" has both narrow and broad definitions (broad = outreach to social services, etc.)
- Jake Pickle research center (police serving citizens, etc.)

- Mindset plays a role—attempting to broaden patrons' ideas of libraries
- Does population size influence *ideas of community*? (i.e., the larger the population, the narrower the focus of *geographic* sense of community)
- People *define* their own communities to define themselves (e.g., culture, age group, school population)
- Community information fair: Refer to school counselor for social services needs (Impetus was parents' questions to librarian. Librarian refers them as a preliminary step to the nurse and the counselor)
- [School's] Community Relations Department [handles requests from parents, community]
- AISD: Community/School Project (inviting people from the community to visit the school, eat lunch in the cafeteria, use the library, get a sense of the school as theirs)

Comment: In some cases, the school IS the public library.

2. Of the following statements, which best fits your situation? For libraries, community information has been defined as:

> A service for providing the community served and individual library users . . . with all pertinent information about and referral to sources that can provide answers to meet their needs for service and assistance. The sources may be government, community, neighborhood or voluntary organizations and institutions, or they may be obtained through the individual. (Jones, Public Library Information and Referral Service. Gaylord, 1978, p. 29).

Do you agree with this definition as it might be applied to school libraries?

A. Definitely yes
B. Yes, generally speaking I agree
C. No, I generally do not agree with this definition
D. No, I most certainly do not agree with this definition
E. Unsure, I really have no opinion on this matter

RESPONSES:

- Curricular connection
- Parents unaware of community resources [available in the library]
- Diversity attracts diversity

3. With the exception of local newspapers, do you provide community information in your library? If so, what kinds?

A. Printed materials such as locally produced pamphlets, brochures, maps
B. Materials from the Internet and World Wide Web
C. Other types

RESPONSES:

- Curriculum connection
- Parents unaware of community resources

4. How do you organize your community information?

    A. No organization is used, this material is so short-lived that we just discard it when it becomes dated.

    B. We generally place it in the vertical or information file with subject headings

    C. We design web pages of community information for the library and/ or school website

RESPONSES:

- Vertical file is going out of style—not used much any more
- Kiosks
- Bulletin board
- Newsletter announcements (public library)
- Email service to refer patrons to external services (public library)

5. How do you provide access to your community information?

    A. Generally it's by conversation or word of mouth

    B. Through the vertical file

    C. Mostly we post it on bulletin boards or give it out at a distribution center in the library

    D. We provide it through links on our website

    E. We provide telephone reference for this type of inquiry on a regular basis

RESPONSES:

- Issue of condoning/promoting sites by having them listed on the library's web page
- You can list information; however, parents' argument is that if you have pamphlets on services, then you are *endorsing* that service
- Parents' newsletters
- Email forwarding [of announcements received by the library]
- Recommending sources or listing commercial sites as open (APL)
- Selection policy highlights certain sites

6. What types of information do you find that you need in your library?

    A. Contact and access information (to businesses, persons, institutions)

    B. Information about cultural events in our community

    C. Medical and social support information

D. Information about government regulations other than school regulations
E. Information about school law, district policies and procedures
F. Information about recreation and entertainment activities
G. Other
H. None of the above

RESPONSES:

- Parenting information
- Unbiased information
- Programming at public library
- Medicaid: this information is not distributed by the state
- Issue: Information is only useful *when it's needed*
- Blood drive notices
- Insurance for kids (uninsured kids)
- Information must be offered in a number of different ways (e.g., e-mail, website)
- Send information to community association e-mail list services
- Calls from people in schools to APL: Librarians must refer them to the correct library sources
- Bilingual story time (APL)
- E-mail is the vehicle of choice to provide information
- Upper grades (middle school, high school) have police officers, social workers
- Community bulletin boards for lost animals, selling cars, etc.
- You need different vehicles to disseminate information (multiple sources); e.g., website, vertical file, paper

7. Looking back at requests for community information you've had within the last two years, which of the following groups represents your most frequent inquirers?

A. Students
B. Teachers
C. Parents
D. Administrators
E. School staff
F. Persons from the community
G. Others
H. None of the above

RESPONSES:

- Parents are by far the biggest group of requesters

- A few persons from the community; not many. Most want to volunteer their services in the schools
- Parents can check out books from school libraries (non-students)
- Printed list of book titles available on the web
- Current issues and topics (e.g., "How to Cope with War") are linked to the library catalog
- "311" service offered by the police department often gets reference-type requests. If they have the information, they give it, or they will refer questions to library services
- Inquiries about animal rescue services
- "Networking"? Do you have community groups coming to you? If so, suggest "VIP" card for seniors in the community (AISD). Card allows users access to:

—School gym
—Discount meals in the cafeteria
—Computers
—Library services
—ESL training classes

- Requests for information on where to take the GED

8. In terms of establishing and maintaining community information in the school library, what are its greatest strengths?

   A. Provides a useful service
   B. Helps students understand how to live in the world
   C. Is useful in promoting learning and student academic achievement
   D. Is especially useful in promoting critical thinking and information literacy skills
   E. Will add depth to the curriculum
   F. Other
   G. None of the above

RESPONSES:

- Surveying parents to find out what skills are available in the community [volunteer pool]
- Curriculum connection, but not particularly via links to community services due to school district policy
- Survey document: Provides a list of "other" teachers of different subjects in the community

9. When considering community information services for the school library, of the following, which one is most problematic for you?

   A. It's very time-consuming to establish and maintain
   B. There is very little demand for it in my school

    C. It would not do much to promote the overall mission and goals of our school

    D. We would not have administrative support for such a program

    E. Community information is too hard to evaluate, opening us up to censorship attempts

    F. Other

    G. None of the Above

RESPONSES:

- Cost/insurance liability/staffing/security
- Cost of overtime and associated costs
- Administration tells the librarian to "use your own judgment" regarding types of materials
- Search time to find appropriate grade-level links (materials/topics appropriate for age group)
- Server/technical restrictions (e.g., size limitations)
- Web page maintenance takes time (resource issue)
- Paper vs. electronic format: which is most effective?

10. At this point, does someone on your staff have the skills to maintain community information on the library's or school's website?

    A. Yes

    B. No

    C. Not sure and really have no way of knowing

RESPONSES:

- Dynix software provides a template for community services information
- Yes, technical facilitator on campus (web page originally set up by school librarian)
- School library generally links to public library website

11. Have you ever been in a school library that had an active community information program?

    A. Yes

    B. No

    C. Not sure and really have no way of knowing

RESPONSES:

- Does information literacy include community information? Yes, we teach students problem-solving skills so that they can go to sources on their own to find information, BUT, since it is not part of the curriculum, it isn't taught in class.
- People [from the community] should be comfortable going into schools

12. Can you recommend a school library that now maintains an active community information program? This can be through a website or other means of access.

   A. Yes (if yes, could we identify the library)
   B. No

RESPONSES:

- Wired for Youth (APL): Children go out into the community to talk to (interact with) people in the community
- Connections Resource Center (http://www.connectionscenter.org/site/PageServer)

SECTION 2. SURVEY QUESTIONNAIRE

DISTRIBUTED SUMMER AND FALL 2003
COMMUNITY INFORMATION FOR SCHOOL LIBRARIES

1. Most of my library work experiences have been in:

   1. School libraries
   2. Public libraries
   3. Academic libraries
   4. Special or corporate libraries
   5. Other

2. Which of the following definitions of community are you most comfortable with:

   1. Community is defined by geographic boundaries
   2. Community is more a state of the mind, an image
   3. For libraries, community information has been defined as:

      A service for providing the community served and individual library users . . . with all pertinent information about and referral to sources that can provide answers to meet their needs for service and assistance. The sources may be government, community, neighborhood or voluntary organizations and institutions, or they may be obtained through the individual. (Jones, *Public Library Information and Referral Service.* Gaylord, 1978, p. 29).

3. Do you agree with this definition as it might be applied to school libraries?

   1. Definitely yes
   2. Yes, generally speaking I agree
   3. No, I generally do not agree with the definition
   4. No, I most certainly do not agree with this definition
   5. Unsure, I really have no opinion on this matter

4. With the exception of local newspapers, and based on limited resources generally available, do you feel school libraries should provide community information in libraries in your community?

   1. Yes
   2. No
   3. Never considered the idea
   4. Unsure

5. If you answered yes to number 4, which *one* of the services listed below seems to be the most important to provide taking into account limited resources?

   1. Printed materials such as locally produced pamphlets, brochures, maps
   2. Local links to available community information on the Internet
   3. A local community information file (directory)
   4. A community bulletin board where items of interests are posted
   5. Closed-circuit television system in school where community information is distributed
   6. Local, printed directories and reference items of local interest
   7. A vertical file of community information
   8. All of the above

6. In terms of establishing and maintaining community information in the school library, which one of the following statements seems best to describe its greatest strength?

   1. Provides a useful information service
   2. Helps students understand how to live in the world
   3. Is useful in promoting learning and student academic achievement
   4. Is especially useful in promoting critical thinking and information literacy skills
   5. Will add depth to the curriculum
   6. None of the above

7. When considering community information services for the school library, which *one* of the following statements seems to best reflect problems?

   1. It is very time-consuming to establish and maintain
   2. There is very little demand for it in most schools
   3. It would not do much to promote the overall mission and goals of schools in my community
   4. Schools in my community would not have administrative support for such a program
   5. Community information is too hard to evaluate, opening up censorship attempts and controversy
   6. None of the above

8. At this point, in general do you feel that the school library staff in your community has the skills to maintain community information on a library's or school's website?

   1. Yes
   2. No
   3. Not sure, and really have no way of knowing

9. Have you ever been in a school library that had an active community information program?

   1. Yes
   2. No
   3. Not sure, and really have no way of knowing

10. Can you recommend a school library that now maintains an active community information program? This can be through a website or other means of access.

    1. Yes (If yes, please identify the library by writing the name and location here.)

    _____

    2. No

11. If you have other comments to provide us with regarding community information in the school, please do so in the space below.

Comments:

For survey staff:

Geographic area code _____

Brake's Community Information Questionnaire

The Need to Know?

Name:

Are you: Male ☐   Female ☐

Are you satisfied with the way you spend your leisure time?

How important are the following in the way you spend your leisure time?

		VERY IMPORTANT	IMPORTANT	NOT IMPORTANT
a.	Your parents	☐	☐	☐
b.	Your own interests	☐	☐	☐
c.	The weather	☐	☐	☐
d.	The facilities available (playing fields, cinemas, etc.)	☐	☐	☐
e.	Money	☐	☐	☐

(*continued*)

Source: Brake, Terence. *The Need to Know: Teaching the Importance of Information.* Final Report for the Period January 1978—March 1978. Published by permission of the British Library.

f.   Jobs at home (looking after brothers, sisters, etc.)   ☐   ☐   ☐

g.   Part-time work   ☐   ☐   ☐

h.   Transport   ☐   ☐   ☐

i.   Religion   ☐   ☐   ☐

j.   Being a girl/Being a boy   ☐   ☐   ☐

Which of these is the most important?

Approximately how many hours would you spend:

		WEEK DAYS	WEEK ENDS
a.	Watching TV		
b.	Listening to the radio		
c.	In youth clubs		
d.	Discos		
e.	Pubs		
f.	Cinemas		
g.	Playing musical instruments		
h.	Listening to records		
I.	Reading		
j.	Playing sports		
k.	Watching sports		
l.	Hobbies		
m.	Games (cards, chess, etc.)		
n.	Visiting libraries, museums		

Film Night

Last Saturday, down at the Street Market, you managed to earn yourself £5. Although at first you couldn't make up your mind how to spend it, you've decided that this coming Saturday you'll visit a 'posh' cinema in London's West End.

What do you need to know?

1. What films are on?

Choose a film:

Where did you find this information?

Remember the law says that if you are under a certain age then you may not be able to see some films.

Is your film rated as a X, AA, A, or U (American G, PGR, X)?

Does the law say that you can see this film?   Yes   No

Where did you find this information?

2. Having chosen a film then you want to know the cinema(s) in which it is showing.

Choose a cinema:

Name_____

Address_____

_____

Telephone Number_____

Where did you find this information?

3. Prices vary according to cinema. How much does it cost to see your film?

£	p

Where did you find this information?

(continued)

4. You don't want to miss the beginning of the film and neither do you want to miss the last bus or tube—it could be a long, long walk.

    At what time does the film start?   [   ]

    And end?   [   ]

Where did you find this information?

[   ]

5. Having decided what you would like to see, then you have to decide how you are going to travel to and from the cinema. By using maps and timetables and whatever you can find, decide on which of the following you will use:

    Bus   [   ]

    Taxi   [   ]

    Ride from Friend   [   ]

6. Where do you depart from?

[   ]

And where do you arrive at?

[   ]

7. In order not to miss the beginning of the film, at what time do you have to catch your first bus or ride?

[   ]

Coming home, when is your last bus or ride?

[   ]

Can you figure out how much it will cost to get to the cinema and back?

£	p

Selected Bibliography

American Association of School Librarians and Association for Educational Communications and Technology. *Information Literacy Standards for Student Learning*. Chicago: American Library Association, 1998.

——. *Information Power: Building Partnerships for Learning*. Chicago: American Library Association, 1998.

——. *Information Power: Guidelines for School Library Media Programs*. Chicago: American Library Association, 1988.

Bajjaly, Stephen. *The Librarian's Community Network Handbook*. Chicago: American Library Association, 1999.

Barclay, Donald A. *Managing Public Access Computers: A How-to-Do-It Manual for Librarians*. New York: Neal-Schuman, 2000.

Barnett, Andy. *Libraries, Community, and Technology*. Jefferson, N.C.: McFarland, 2002.

Blank, Mary Ann, and Cheryl Kershaw. *Designbook for Building Partnerships: School, Home, and Community*. Lancaster, Pa.: Technomic, 1998.

Booth, Andrew, and Anne Brice, eds. *Evidence-Based Practice for Information Professionals: A Handbook*. London: Facet, 2003.

Bowditch, George. *Cataloging Photographs: A Procedure for Small Collections*. Rev. ed. Nashville, Tenn.: American Association for State and Local History, 1975.

Bradburn, Frances Bryant. *Output Measures for School Library Media Programs*. New York: Neal-Schuman, 1999.

Brake, Terence. *The Need to Know: Teaching the Importance of Information*. Final Report for the Period January 1978–March 1978. London: British Library, 1980.

Breivik, Patricia Senn. *Student Learning in an Information Age.* Phoenix: Oryx Press, 1998.

Brill, Naomi I. *Working with People: The Helping Process.* 8th ed. Boston: Pearson/Allyn & Bacon, 2005.

Chowdhury, G. G., and Susatta Chowdhury. *Introduction to Digital Libraries.* New York: Neal-Schuman, 2002.

Childers, Thomas. *Information and Referral: Public Libraries.* Norwood, N.J.: Ablex, 1984.

Churchill, Gilbert A., and J. Paul Peter. *Marketing: Creating Value for Customers.* 2nd ed. Boston: Irwin/McGraw-Hill, 1998.

Clinton, Hillary R. *It Takes a Village: And Other Lessons Children Teach Us.* New York: Simon & Schuster, 1996.

Costello, Joan, and others. "Promoting Public Library Partnerships with Youth Agencies." *Journal of Youth Services in Libraries* 15(Fall 2001): 8–15.

———. *School Libraries and the Electronic Community: The Internet Connection.* Lanham, Md.: Scarecrow, 1997.

Cooke, Alison. *Neal-Schuman Authoritative Guide to Evaluating Information on the Internet.* New York: Neal-Schuman, 1999.

Craver, Kathleen W. *School Library Media Centers in the 21st Century: Changes and Challenges.* Westport, Conn.: Greenwood Press, 1994.

Cylde, Laurel A. *Managing InfoTech in School Library Media Centers.* Englewood, Colo.: Libraries Unlimited, 1999.

Czopek, Vanessa. *The Vertical File.* Staff Report. Mesa, AZ.: Mesa Arizona Public Library, 1986. ERIC Reproduction Document No. ED 275 344.

De Sáez, Eileen Elliott. *Marketing Concepts for Libraries and Information Services.* 2nd ed. London: Facet, 2002.

Dillon, Andrew. *Designing Usable Electronic Text.* 2nd ed. New York: Taylor & Francis, 2003.

———. *Designing Usable Electronic Text.* 2nd ed. Boca Raton, Fla.: CRC Press, 2004.

Doggett, Sandra L. *Beyond the Book: Technology Integration into the Secondary School Library Media Curriculum,* ed. Paula K. Montgomery. Englewood, Colo.: Libraries Unlimited, 2000.

Donham, Jean. *Enhancing Teaching and Learning: A Leadership Guide for School Media Specialists.* New York: Neal-Schuman, 1998

Dorfman, Diane, and others, *Planning for Youth Success: Resources and Training Manual, Connecting Schools, Families, and Communities for Youth Success.* Portland, Ore.: Northwest Regional Educational Laboratory, 2001. ERIC Reproduction No. 459 540.

Drabenstott, Karen Markey. *Subject Access to Visual Resources Collections: A Model for Computer Construction of Thematic Catalogs.* New York: Greenwood Press, 1986.

Durrance, Joan C., and Karen E. Pettigrew. *Online Community Information: Creating a Nexus at Your Library.* Chicago: American Library Association, 2002.

Eisenberg, Michael B., and Robert E. Berkowitz. *Teaching Information and Technology Skills: The Big6 in Elementary Schools.* Worthington, Ohio: Linworth, 1999.

Eisenberg, Michael B., and others. *Information Literacy: Essential Skills for the Information Age.* 2nd ed. Westport, Conn.: Libraries Unlimited, 2004.

Evans, G. Edward. *Developing Library and Information Center Collections.* 4th ed. Englewood, Colo.: Libraries Unlimited, 2000.

Evans, Hilary. *Picture Librarianship.* New York: K. G. Saur, 1980.

Everhart, Nancy. *Evaluating the School Library Media Center: Analysis Techniques and Research Practices.* Englewood, Colo.: Libraries Unlimited, 1998.

Farmer, Lesley S. J. *Student Success and Library Media Programs: A Systems Approach to Research and Best Practice.* Westport, Conn.: Libraries Unlimited, 2003.

———. *Teaching with Opportunity: Media Programs, Community Constituencies and Technology.* Englewood Colo.: Libraries Unlimited, 2001.

Farmer, Lesley S. J., and Will Fowler. *More Than Information: The Role of the Library Media Center in the Multimedia Classroom.* Worthington, Ohio: Linworth, 1999.

Fleming, Malcolm L., and W. Howard Levie, eds. *Instructional Message Design Principles from the Behavioral and Cognitive Sciences.* 2nd ed. Englewood Cliffs, N.J.: Educational Technology Publications, 1993.

Flowers, Helen F. *Public Relations for School Media Library Programs: 500 Ways to Influence People and Win Friends for Your School Library Media Center.* New York: Neal-Schuman, 1998.

Fountain, Joanna F. *Subject Headings for School and Public Libraries: An LCSH Companion.* 3rd ed. Englewood, Colo.: Libraries Unlimited, 2001.

Gilchrist, Alan, and Barry Mahon. *Information Architecture: Designing Information Environments for Purpose.* New York: Neal-Schuman, 2004.

Gorman, G. E., and Ruth H. Miller, eds. *Collection Management for the 21st Century: A Handbook for Librarians.* Westport, Conn.: Greenwood Press, 1997.

Gorman, Michael. *Our Enduring Values: Librarianship in the 21st Century.* Chicago: American Library Association, 2000.

Graham, Lisa. *Basics of Design: Layout and Typography for Beginners.* Albany, N.Y.: Delmar, 2002.

———. *The Principles of Interactive Design.* Albany, N.Y.: Delmar, 1999.

Gregory, Vicki L., and others. *Multicultural Resources on the Internet: The United States and Canada.* Englewood, Colo.: Libraries Unlimited, 1999.

———. *Selecting and Managing Electronic Resources: A How-to-Do-It Manual.* New York: Neal-Schuman, 2000.

Hahn, Doyne M. "Vertical File Selection Policy and Procedure Policy Manual." Unpublished Guide, Ball State University, 1986. ERIC Reproduction No. 283 582.

Hart, Thomas L. *The School Library Media Facilities Planner: A Multimedia Guide with Specifications, Color Diagrams and Short Videos.* New York: Neal-Schuman, 2004.

Hawthorne, Karen, and Jane E. Gibson. *Bulletin Boards and 3-D Showcases That Capture Them with Pizzazz.* Englewood, Colo.: Libraries Unlimited, 1999.

Haycock, Ken, ed. *Foundations for Effective School Library Media Programs.* Englewood, Colo.: Libraries Unlimited, 1999.

Heinich, Robert, and others. *Instructional Media and Technologies for Learning.* 7th ed. Upper Saddle River, N.J.: Merrill, 2002.

Hennepin County Public Library, *Cataloging Bulletin, 1973 to present.* See also their *Library Cumulative Authority List,* 1993.

Hiatt-Michael, Diana B. ed. *Promising Practices to Connect Schools with the Community*. Greenwich, Conn.: Information Age Publishing, 2003.

Hughes, Lorna M. *Digitizing Collections: Strategic Issues for the Information Manager*. New York: Neal-Schuman, 2004.

Hunter, Gregory S. *Developing and Maintaining Practical Archives: A How-to-Do-It Manual*. 2nd ed. New York: Neal-Schuman, 2003.

Illick, Joseph E. *American Childhoods*. Philadelphia: University of Pennsylvania Press, 2002.

Illinois Library Association. *The Internet and Our Children: A Community Partnership*. Chicago: Illinois Library Association, 2000.

Introduction to Art Image Access: Issues, Tools, Standards, Strategies, ed. Murtha Baca. Los Angles: Getty Research Institute, 2002.

Johnson, Peggy, and Bonnie MacEwan, eds. *Virtually Yours: Models for Managing Electronic Resources and Services*. Chicago: American Library Association, 1999.

Katz, Bill, ed. *New Technologies and Reference Services*. New York: Haworth Press, 2000.

Kearney, Carol A. *Curriculum Partner: Redefining the Role of the Library Media Specialists*. Westport, Conn.: Greenwood Press, 2000.

Kohn, Rita T., and Krysta A.Tepper. *Have You Got What They Want? Public Relations Strategies for the School Librarian/Media Specialist: A Reference Tool*. 2nd ed. Metuchen, N.J.: Scarecrow, 1990.

Kravitz, Nancy. *Censorship and the School Library Media Center*. Westport, Conn.: Libraries Unlimited, 2002.

Kuhlthau, Carol Collier, and others, eds. *The Virtual School Library: Gateway to the Information Superhighway*. Englewood, Colo.: Libraries Unlimited, 1996.

Loertscher, David V. *Collection Mapping in the LMC: Building Access in a World of Technology*. Castle Rock: Colo.: Hi Willow Research, 1996.

Loertscher, David V., and others. *Building a School Library Collection Plan: A Beginning Handbooks with Internet Assist*. San Jose, Calif.: Hi Willow Research, 1999.

Loertscher, David V., and Blanche Woolls. *Information Literacy: A Review of the Research*. San Jose, Calif.: Hi Willow Research, 1999.

Lukenbill, W. Bernard. *Collection Development for a New Century in the School Library Media Center*. Westport, Conn.: Greenwood Press, 2002.

———. "Community Information in Schools: An Operational Approach and Model." *The Reference Librarian* 21 (1988). Reprinted in *Information and Referral in Reference Services*, eds. M. S. Middleton and Bill Katz. New York: Haworth Press, 1988.

Lushington, Nolan. *Libraries Designed for Users: A 21st Century Guide*. New York: Neal-Schuman, 2002.

MARC 21 Format for Community Information; Including Guidelines for Content Designation. Prepared by Network Development and MARC Standards Office, Library of Congress in cooperation with Standards and support, National Library of Canada, 1999 ed. Washington, D.C.: Library of Congress; Ottawa: National Library of Canada, 1999.

Markless, Sharon, and David Streatfield. *Evaluating the Impact of Your Library*. London: Facet, 2004.

Martinez, Anne. *Cheap Web Tricks!: Build and Promote a Successful Web Site Without Spending a Dime*. New York: Osborne/McGraw-Hill, 2001.

Michel, George J. *Building Schools: The New School and Community Relations*. Lancaster, Pa.: Technomic, 1997.

Minkel, Walter, and Roxanne Hsu Feldman. *Delivering Web Reference Services to Young People*. Chicago: American Library Association, 1999.

Nichols, Mary Anne. *Merchandising Library Materials to Young Adults*. Greenwood Village, Colo.: Libraries Unlimited, 2002.

Orna, Elizabeth. *Information Strategies in Practice*. Burlington, Vt.: Gower, 2004.

———. *Practical Information Policies*. 2nd ed. Brookefield, Vt.: Gower, 1999.

Owen, Jane C., and Martha N. Ovando. *A Superintendent's Guide to Creating Community*. Lanham, Md.: Scarecrow, 2000.

Pantry, Sheila. *Building Community Information Networks: Strategies and Experiences*. London: Library Association, 1999.

Peck, Robert S. *Libraries, the First Amendment and Cyberspace: What You Need to Know*. Chicago: American Library Association, 2000.

Peterson, Bryan L. *Design Basics for Creative Results*. Rev. 1st ed. Cincinnati, Ohio: How Design Books, 2003.

Pettigrew, Karen E., and others. "Facilitating Community Information Seeking Using the Internet. Findings from Three Public Library Community Network Systems." *Journal of the American Society for Information Science and Technology* 53 (September 2002).

Public Library Association. *Guidelines for Establishing Community Information and Referral Services in Public Libraries*, 4th ed. Chicago: American Library Association, 1997.

Robl, Ernest H. *Organizing Your Photographs*. New York: Amphoto, 1986.

Ross, Ann, and Karen Olsen. *The Way We Were ... The Way We Can Be: A Vision for the Middle School Through Integrated Thematic Instruction*. 2nd ed. Village of Oak Creek, Ariz.: Susan Kovalik & Associates, 1993.

Sarason, Seymour B. *The Psychological Sense of Community: Prospects for a Community Psychology*. 1st ed. San Francisco: Jossey-Bass, 1974.

Savich, Chanelle McMillan. "The State of the Vertical File in DuPage County, Illinois, Public High School Libraries." Unpublished Student Research Paper, Northern Illinois University, 1993. ED Reproduction No. 375 853.

Song, Yuwu. *Building Better Web Sites: A How-to-Do-It Manual for Librarians*. New York: Neal-Schuman, 2003.

Spool, Jared M., and others. *Web Site Usability: A Designer's Guide*. San Francisco: Morgan Kaufmann, 1999.

Stallard, Charles K., and Julie Cocker. *The Promise of Technology in Schools: The Next 20 Years*. Lanham, Md.: Scarecrow, 2001.

Stielow, Frederick, ed. *Creating a Virtual Library: A How-To-Do-It Manual*. New York: Neal-Schuman, 1999.

Stripling, Barbara K., ed. *Learning and Libraries in an Information Age: Principles and Practice*. Englewood, Colo.: Libraries Unlimited, 1999.

Stripling, Barbara K., and Sandra Hughes-Hassell, eds. *Curriculum Connections through the Library*. Westport, Conn.: Libraries Unlimited, 2003.

Thomas, Nancy P. *Information Literacy and Information Skills Instruction: Applying Research to Practice in the School Library Media Center*, ed. Paula Kay; Montgomery. Englewood, Colo.: Libraries Unlimited, 1999.

Toronto Public Libraries. *Subject Headings for Vertical Files.* 2nd ed. Toronto: The
     Library, 1971.
Trotta, Carmine J., and Marcia Trotta, *The Librarian's Facility Management Hand-
     book.* New York: Neal-Schuman, 2001.
United Way of America. *Measuring Program Outcomes: A Practical Approach.*
     Alexandria, Va.: United Way of America, 1996.
Van Orden, Phyllis J., and Kay Bishop. *The Collection Program in Schools: Concepts
     Practices and Information Sources.* 3rd ed. Englewood, Colo.: Libraries Un-
     limited, 2001.
Walter, Virginia. A. *Children and Libraries: Getting It Right.* Chicago: American
     Library Association, 2001.
Walters, Susanne. *Library Marketing That Works: A How-to-Do-It Manual.* 1st ed.
     New York: Neal-Schuman, 2003.
Weisner, Stan. *Information Is Empowering: Developing Public Library Services for
     Youth at Risk.* Edited by Katie Scarborough. 2nd ed. Oakland, Calif.: Bay
     Area Library and Information System, 1992.
Whitesides, William L. *Reinvention of the Public Library for the 21st Century.*
     Englewood, Colo.: Libraries Unlimited, 1998.
Wileman, Ralph E. *Visual Communicating.* Englewood Cliffs, N.J.: Educational
     Technology Publications, 1993.
Woolls, Blanche. *The School Library Media Manager.* 2nd ed. Englewood, Colo.:
     Libraries Unlimited, 1999.
Yakel, Elizabeth. *Starting an Archives.* Metuchen, N.J.: Society of American Archivists
     and Scarecrow Press, 1994.

What's In a Name?

In considering the many challenges associated with the idea of community information programs, I was continually met with how to refer to the school library media center. The profession has long attempted to replace the name *school library* with *school library media center*. The name does not appear to be widely accepted beyond the borders of the United States and Canada. The term *teacher-librarian* is preferred in many other English-speaking countries, but school library media specialist is the form preferred by the style directives of this publisher. American and Canadian professional writers and authorities appear to have accepted this term with little reservation.

Nevertheless, this is a name that has not been altogether accepted by the general public. A recent article in the *Austin American Statesman* indicated that the name was part of educational jargonese, and the writer marginalized it to the realm of terms to be overlooked and soon forgotten. In 2003, the State Board for Educator Certification (SBEC), the official board charged with certification of school professional personnel in Texas and supported by the school library media professionals, discarded its two levels of certification for Learning Resources Specialists and now certifies only under the name School Librarian. Serving two masters is an impossible task, so in the writing of this book, I may have blundered from time to time by using school librarian and school library when referring to the school library media specialist and the school library media center. But such is life.

Index

About the Author

W. BERNARD LUKENBILL is Professor, School of Information, University of Texas at Austin.